From "Blues" to Bliss

ROBERT L. THORNTON
Co-author DIANNE HALL

From "Blues" to Bliss,
a sequel to Twenty-Seven-Eighty Blues.

*With memoirs, anecdotes and vignettes I share my forty plus
years of bliss with one of the most talented and amazing
women of her generation.*

ISBN 10: 1-933817-74-7
ISBN 13: 978-1-933817-74-3

Published by Profits Publishing
http://profitspublishing.com

Canadian Address

1265 Charter Hill Drive
Coquitlam, BC, V3E 1P1
Phone: (604) 941-3041
Fax: (604) 944-7993

US Address

1300 Boblett Street
Unit A-218
Blaine, WA 98230
Phone: (866) 492-6623
Fax: (250) 493-6603

To the memory of my loving wife

MARTHA THORNTON

a quiet, trailblazing pioneer, Hall of Fame recipient[*]

… and the love of my life.

*Chicago Sun Times, October 1, 1993.

Acknowledgements

"Michigan Bell's first hire in a new college graduate program was Martha Hall. Bright, quick, articulate and attractive, she had to convince those that worked for her that she could learn their job and supervise them in a manner that helped them as well as herself. She was very successful! So successful, in fact, that we hired several more just like her. The program was so right for the times. It was not easy for her, however. She was the Jackie Robinson of the traffic department. The very first one is a true trailblazer. She accomplished that, however, and went on to be promoted time after time. It was amazing to watch her maintain her poise and self-confidence in job after job with new responsibilities and expectations rising with each new position. I worked closely with her during all of these years and never saw her be down or complain or question her peers. Amazing when you think about her working in a new, totally male environment. She kept her female charm without once ever asking for favors, performing all of her responsibilities that all of her male peers did without complaint. She was highly respected and admired by her workers, her peers and supervisors. And, I might

add, she accomplished all of this while maintaining a keen sense of humor—and never without a smile!"

Frank Zimmerman
Former Vice President of Ameritech and
former President of the Illinois Bell Telephone
Company

"I never, ever, met a person in my 37 years at Ameritech and the Bell system that possessed more integrity than Martha. She was my role model—the person I would go to with my deepest concerns and my need for advice. She was always right on target with her wisdom and her answers. I loved working with her and I will always be grateful for her incredible insights. God created a very special lady—I was so fortunate to know her and to work with her; you were the most fortunate of all—to deeply love her, to be her soul mate and to be her husband. She adored you, and I am sure she continues to this day to feel blessed to have been your wife."

Dennis Johnson
Former Vice President of Ameritech

At the conclusion of an interview regarding my first book, Twenty-Seven-Eighty Blues, the reporter asked me if I was going to write another book. Thinking the interview was over, my response was, "I don't know, I may write one about my wife."

When the interview came out in print it said 'I was going to write a book about my wife.' After reading this, her many friends started calling.

The first was a longtime friend of both of ours,

and a very important mentor of mine while I was writing the Blues.

He said that somebody should write a book about Martha and that I was the best one to do it ... a very special thanks to you ... Frank Zimmerman.

Mr. Z's call was followed by others, all with similar messages. I want to thank all of you for your faith and support.

A special thanks to you and your family ... Dennis and Karen Johnson. I want you all to know how much you're many telephone calls and e-mails have meant to me.

Judy Johnson, my editor and good friend ... you did it again. First it was 'Annie' and now From "Blues" to Bliss. *I could never have done this without you.*

And last, but not least, a very special thanks to my Co-Author and daughter ... Dianne Hall. I don't know what I would do without you.

Robert L. Thornton

Author's Note

MY FATHER LOST HIS JOB DURING THE GREAT DEPRESSION and our family of five plunged head over heels into poverty. We lived in Detroit, Michigan and I was seven years old. The next eight years were very grim indeed. I can recall a government nurse coming to our house and, among other things just as ridiculous, suggesting that my mother add water to our milk to make it go further.

I can still see a vision of my father cutting cardboard innersoles for our hole-ridden shoes. I don't know how many times I saw him come home practically freezing to death from standing in lines all day long looking for work.

Although I was oblivious to the event at the time, a miracle happened during those depression years that would someday make me so grateful to have survived them and the terrible war that followed. I was eleven years old on February 1, 1936, when a beautiful baby girl was born in Detroit to a proud housepainter and his wife. After having two boys, they joyfully named their first daughter Martha Lucille.

Things finally improved for my family in 1940 when my father was called back to work, and we then moved to a modest home of our own on Detroit's east side. But a damper was put on our newfound prosperity when, in 1941, the Japanese bombed Pearl Harbor and America suddenly was at war.

In 1942 my brother Glen, the oldest sibling, was the first to leave home. He joined the Army Air Corps and became a navigator on the B17 'Flying Fortress.'

In 1943 I dropped out of Denby High School, on Detroit's east side, to join the Army Air Corps and became a radio operator mechanic gunner on a B17 combat crew.

My younger brother, Wayne, joined the paratroopers in 1944. With all three boys in the service, sister Joan was the only sibling left at home.

Brother Glen, stationed in England, flew 35 missions over Germany with the 8th Air Force, and then flew 22 missions on B29s, the 'Super Fortress,' over North Korea in that war. A shell fired by a Chinese MIG exploded in the radar room and cut the artery in his left arm, earning him the purple heart to go along with his many air medals. He regained the use of his arm, but never regained the feeling in his left thumb.

While Brother Wayne was sitting on Okinawa waiting to jump over Japan, the first Atomic bombs were dropped, which, in all probability, saved his life. The paratroops were expecting 80 percent casualties if they had to jump over Japan. Wayne ended his career and returned home after spending several years with the occupation forces in Japan.

At nineteen, I survived 27 combat missions over Germany, also in the 8th Army Air Corps. On May 8, 1945, seven days before my twentieth birthday, the war in Europe ended. Then my Squadron, the 325th of the 92nd Bomb Group, moved from the Podington Air Base in England to an air base near Istres, France. At the same time the 92nd 327th Squadron moved to Oran, North Africa.

Since the war in the Pacific was still going on and we knew nothing about the role the atom bombs would soon play, we had every reason to believe that we were going to invade Japan. To that end, the powers that be wanted General Patton's troops moved from Europe to the Pacific as soon as possible.

The 325th Squadron was assigned the job of transporting General Patton's troops to Casablanca, North Africa on the first leg of their journey to the Pacific. The Air Force stripped some B17s down of guns and turrets and installed benches on each side of the aircraft from the radio room back to the tail. With no gunners, we became a five-man crew, consisting of a Pilot, Co-pilot, Navigator, Engineer and Radio man.

Each aircraft could carry 37 men per trip. Flying out of Istres we made the five-and-a-half=hour flight to Casablanca and dropped Patton's men off there, then turned the plane around and flew to an American naval air base nearby where we spent the night.

The 327th, already in Africa, then flew Patton's men to the Azores on the next leg of their journey. The next morning we flew French Jews, who had fled France to avoid the Nazi death camps during the war, back to their homeland. The 325th made two "round robin" trips to Africa each week for the next seven months. The Army had a name for everything, and they called this operation "The Green Project."

***

On Friday, December 14, 1945, the RMS Queen Mary anchored off the shores of Hoboken, New Jersey. She had just arrived from Southampton, England with 14,000 American WWII veterans on board. Because the prevailing winds prevented the ship from entering the harbor, the vets had to climb down rope ladders to waiting ferry boats with everything they owned in duffle bags slung over their shoulders. At the dock, Red Cross girls welcomed the returning vets home with small cartons of milk. These vets were on their way home at long last. There were no fanfares or ticker tape parades, just milk.

I, 20-year-old Tech/Sergeant Robert L. Thornton, was on the Queen Mary that day. In my book, *Twenty-Seven-Eighty Blues*, which I will sometimes now refer to as just the "Blues," I recounted my memoirs of WWII that had such a deep and enduring influence on my life. But my story did not end there. In fact, it was just the beginning of the unfolding of my destiny.

After I was discharged, I went home to Detroit. With tens of thousands of returning vets hitting the job market, employment was hard to come by. Finally, after weeks of pounding the pavement, because of my service background with radio equipment, I landed a job with the Western Electric Companies Installation Organization, a subsidiary of AT&T.

The "marriage market" was also saturated with eager vets anxious to make up for lost time in starting a family. I was one of those vets too; however, this story is not about my failed first marriage. It is about my second, an incredibly successful one.

This story of *From "Blues" to Bliss* begins shortly after I took over the job of Employment and Training for the Western Electric Installation Organization in the state of Michigan. Not long after I started that job, the company dramatically changed its hiring practices. Previous to this change all Western Electric Installers were exclusively white males. Then, for the first time in the company's history, Western Electric's ads for employment read that they were an "Equal Opportunity Employer."

These changes took place shortly after the landmark decision of the Supreme Court in 1954, Brown v. the Board of Education, which triggered a decade of racial unrest. This decision found that state laws establishing separate public schools for black and white students were unconstitutional.

Then, in 1955, Rosa Parks was arrested for refusing to give up her seat on a bus to a white passenger. This act led to the desegregation of interstate travel facilities.

On June 10, 1963, John Kennedy signed the Equal Pay Act (EPA).

On June 12, 1963, Medgar Evers, a black field secretary for the NAACP, was murdered outside his home in Jackson, Mississippi.

On August 28, 1963, Martin Luther King, Jr. delivered his famous 'I Have a Dream' speech.

On November 11, 1963, President Kennedy was assassinated and Vice President Lyndon Johnson became president.

On December 16, 1963, the Michigan Bell Telephone Company made history by hiring their first female college graduate into a management position. Her name was Martha Hall.

There are some who believe that Kennedy's Equal Pay Act, followed by the Congressional Equal Employment Opportunity Commission (EEOC), to some degree influenced AT&T to change its employment practices. However, true or not, Michigan Bell and Ameritech Corporation became the beneficiaries of the new practice, as you shall see.

***

While these events were playing out on the national stage, the pastor of a small Lutheran church that I attended in Macomb County, Michigan negotiated a remarkable agreement with a pastor of an all-black Baptist church in the nearby town of Roseville, Michigan. The two men agreed that our Lutheran congregation would attend a service one Sunday at the Baptist church and the following Sunday the Baptist congregation would attend our service. And that's how I met my good friend Pastor Junior.

This, perhaps coincidently, was about the same time that Western Electric declared that it was an equal opportunity employer. And we thought the non-whites would be knocking our doors down to get in. But that never happened. For at least the first four weeks I never saw one non-white applicant. Then I thought of my friend Pastor Junior, and arranged to meet him in his church. When I asked for his help he readily agreed. As a matter of fact, the very first 'Pastor Junior man' I hired and trained went on one day to also become the very first black supervisor in the Detroit Installation Area.

The following is based on a true story; however, poetic license with scripting had to be used in some conversations where the actual words are long forgotten, but the intent and meanings have endured.

Prologue

Hospice House, Rand Blvd., Sarasota, FL
Friday, October 27, 2006 6:40 a.m.

"SHE'S GONE," I HEARD SOMEONE SAY. I woke up on the couch in room 12 of the Hospice House and saw a nurse and her aid leaning over my wife. I jumped to her side and saw her last breath leave like a sigh.

"She's so beautiful," the nurse said, and they left the room. Leaning over, I kissed her lips for the last time. She *was* beautiful, and looked *so* young.

Stunned … the realization of what had just happened hit me like a ton of bricks. I was in a daze … *my best friend, my precious soul mate and the love of my life, was gone!* I looked at the clock on the wall and saw that the time was 6:40 a.m.

After seven years of watching her valiant fight against cancer one would think that I would have been prepared … but I wasn't. There is *no* way one can prepare for such a horrendous event. I was broken hearted and stricken with grief like never before. There are no words to describe my grief. My one thought was, *"How am I going to go on without her?"* Eleven years older than her, I should have gone first.

Part One

CHAPTER ONE

MY DAY STARTED OUT LIKE SO MANY OTHER MID-WINTER MORNINGS … with me brushing the snow from my car and scraping the ice off of the windows. This was not unusual; in fact, it was commonplace. After all, this *was* Michigan, and in the winter it snows here.

If I had to guess, so far that morning only about one inch of snow had fallen. That was about normal, so if you had not heard a weather report yet you would have had no reason to believe that this day would be any different than most winter days. But little did I know, as I headed for my office in Detroit, that this was going to be one of the worst snow storms to hit the city in years. It was the winter of 1964–65.

On this particular day snow would blanket the city, bringing it to its knees. Every school would close, public transportation would grind to a halt and traffic on most main arteries would snarl and practically come to a stop, but it didn't look that bad at 7:00 a.m. when I pulled into the Michigan Bell Telephone Company's parking lot. So far it looked like it would be just another winter day at the office.

Although I worked for the Western Electric Company, known as WECO for short, I leased space in the telephone office belonging to the Michigan Bell Telephone Company, better known then as MBT. My present job was to hire and train more telephone equipment installers. I preferred a telephone office for my classroom so I could take my students on tours of the building, showing them what they would actually be doing.

In those days, WECO manufactured, installed and tested all of the equipment that went inside a telephone office. When they turned it over to the telephone company to maintain, it was in perfect working condition. As time went by WECO also installed additions and modifications to the equipment.

That day, having been born and raised in Michigan, I was aware of the old saying that if you don't like the weather now, just wait a few minutes. So when I entered the building I just stomped the snow from my feet, got on the elevator as I did every workday and punched "2" for the second floor.

At the same moment a female voice called out …

"Hold the elevator please!"

So I held the door open as a young lady quickly entered while brushing the snow from her coat and stamping *her* feet.

"Thank you so much," she said, as she turned around to face me. And there … standing so close to me I could smell a hint of her tantalizing perfume … was the gorgeous creature I had been admiring from a distance for several weeks now. I was absolutely smitten by her bright smile and the bluest eyes I have ever seen. It was all I could do to keep from embracing her and kissing her beautiful lips right then and there!

Little did we know that, because of this chance encounter on an elevator on this particular day, our lives would never be the same again. I had never felt this way before. ... I'm sure it was love at first sight. I took particular note of her left hand clutching her glove, which, much to my relief, was ring-less. We exchanged comments about the weather, the elevator stopped, and I held the door open for her so she could step out first.

Turning into my office to hang up my coat, I resisted a strange yearning in my heart to follow as she walked down the hall, passed my classroom and entered the operating room ... operating room meaning telephone operators, not surgeons. As I watched the door close behind her I said to myself, "There goes the woman I'm going to marry."

Crossing the hall, I entered the cafeteria for my morning coffee. I knew that most everyone arrived early enough for coffee. It was a social ritual ... morning coffee and chitchat. I felt fairly certain that my future bride would be there after she hung her coat up. So this morning, instead of sitting with someone I knew as I usually did, I sat where I could watch the door, hoping against hope that she would come for coffee this morning and perhaps sit at my table. The only thing running through my head at the moment was the image of that beautiful young lady.

It didn't take long and ... there she was! With her coffee cup in one hand she surveyed the room as if she were looking for someone. When she saw me our eyes locked for a moment; she smiled and waved with her free hand, and then sat down with a group of telephone operators, a scenario I should have expected. But, my thought and hope was that she was looking for me for the same reason I was looking for her. True or not, I believed it was so.

Now I had to find out who this young lady was that I was in love with. That wouldn't be hard, I thought ... I knew her boss, the Chief Operator. I had been in that operating room many times when I was a young installer. Even now I still knew some of the Group Chief Operators in that room. In fact, I had lunch with one of them only a few days ago.

That evening I was sitting at my desk unaware of just how bad the conditions were outside. I had dismissed my students earlier and was finishing up some overdue paperwork. I could hear wind howling outside and snow hitting the window panes behind me. However, that did not alarm me. Aside from my time in the service I had lived my entire life in Michigan and I was not overly concerned with what I thought was just another snow storm.

Putting my pen down, I contemplated where I was going to eat dinner. It had to be a place where I could eat at the bar. Since my wife and I had separated, eating with others at a restaurant bar had become my main social diversion. I hated to eat alone and I hated asking for a table for one. Hopefully, I thought, my divorce would soon be final.

I'd heard about a new steak house near the Oakland Mall I hadn't tried yet, so I thought, 'Why not go there tonight?' I got up, stretched, and decided to cross the hall to the cafeteria for one last cup of coffee before hitting the road ... anything to kill time before going back to my lonely apartment. And, who knows, my future bride may be just across the hall.

Scanning the room on my way to the coffee urn, I spotted the woman of my dreams sitting with the Chief Operator. At first I thought, this was my chance to act … I could go over there, say hello to the Chief, point to an empty chair at their table and ask, 'Do you mind?'

But common sense told me that that was not a good idea. They could be talking business and the Chief might resent being interrupted. So, playing it safe, I sat with Jim Johnson and two of his people.

I did notice that as I sat down my new love saw me, and those beautiful blue eyes again locked on mine, this time for just a little bit longer before she turned her head away … and I almost melted. That was a good sign. It certainly was encouraging. 'What was she thinking about?' I wondered. 'Was she really trying to tell me something with those beautiful eyes?' I wanted so much to think she was. That look was not new to me; in my past life it almost always meant something special.

"Hi Bob. Have you looked outside lately … we're snowed in!" Jim said as I sat down. Jim was the Chief Switchman, and with the exception of the operating room, he ran things around here. I was more interested in what was going on in this room, not outside, but I didn't want Jim to know that.

"I knew it was snowing … but is it that bad?"

"Gratiot's covered with over two feet of snow, it hasn't been plowed yet, there's nothing moving out there, and it's still coming down hard. Maintenance will set a cot up in your office and sandwiches and coffee will be available here all night," Jim said.

'Oh well, so much for that new steak house tonight,' I thought. I now realized that I had grossly misjudged the magnitude of the day's events. Of course I had seen days like this before, but they were very few and far in between.

About twenty people were in the cafeteria that evening when someone poked his head inside and announced that the bar down the street was open. After grabbing our coats and galoshes, most everyone plodded through the snow and into the bar. The bartender … so glad to see us … put some tables together and I sat down expecting to enjoy a most unusual evening. But I had no idea then of just *how* unusual it was going to be.

While sitting at the last chair at the left end of the table with my back to the door, my heart took a leap when my mystery woman surprised me by coming up behind me, and then sat at the very end of the table … right next to me.

I noted that there were lots of other places she could have sat. If I had any doubts of her interest in me it was now gone. What she had just done told me something about her … this beautiful woman had more guts than I did. I was sure that her sitting where she did was no accident.

Before we could say anything, the bartender took our drink orders and disappeared. Then she turned her attention to me.

"Hello … thanks again for holding the elevator for me this morning," she said as she swept some loose hair over one ear. 'What beautiful hands,' I thought, 'this lady is all female' … then she surprised me when she continued.

"Are you Bob Thornton?" I knew that she was new here … most everyone in the operating room knew who I was.

"I am."

"I'm Martha Hall; I work in the operating room."

"It's my pleasure Martha Hall, I'm so glad to meet you. I know where you work, I see you just about every time you go by my office."

All fear of rejection was gone now, the ball was in my court, and at last I knew the name of the woman I wanted so much to marry.

"What do you do in the operating room? You can't be an operator; those that aren't working have no doubt gone home while they could."

"I'm a Group Chief Operator. I was recently transferred here from Lakeview." I was very familiar with Lakeview; it was another telephone office a few miles north of here and I had been there many times.

I knew that a Group Chief Operator was a first-level management position. I also knew that until a little over a year ago the Bell system had taken great pride in promoting from within, but were now hiring a few college graduates into a management training program that we at WECO called 'high risk, high reward.' That meant, if the trainee did not meet the company's performance expectations in a given time period, he, or she, would be terminated. However, if they did meet their expectations they would become first-level managers and would then be competing

*with other managers for future promotions. WECO
had recently instituted the same program.*

*What I did not know at this time was that on
December 16, 1963, Martha Hall was the very first
female Michigan Bell had hired in that new program,
and she was hired after graduating from Wayne State
University 'summa cum laude.' And on June 21, 1964
she had met their expectations and was now a 'bona
fide' Group Chief Operator.*

We spent some time talking about the weather until
the bartender returned with our drinks. After downing
my scotch and water, any edge I might have had
was gone. But then Martha Hall shocked me with a
question I could *never* have anticipated. Out of the
clear blue sky, she asked,

"Are you a skier?"

Taken totally by surprise by the question, I heard
myself say ...

"Yes," even though I had never skied before in
my life ... but what else could I do? If I said no,
and she wanted to go skiing, I may be letting this
opportunity of a lifetime pass me by. *And at any risk
I did not want that to happen.*

I had no way of knowing at that time what would
have happened had I said no, but I thought her
response justified my lie.

"I would like to go skiing this weekend, would
you come with me?"

I could hardly believe what just happened. My
dream girl I had only met today had just asked *me* for
a date. Then I heard myself say ...

"I would love to." And that was no lie!

CHAPTER TWO

SOMETIME LATER, BACK AT MY OFFICE, I WONDERED, 'What will I do when she finds out that I had not told her the truth?' And I knew that she was bound to find out. Then another thing just occurred to me, 'How come this beautiful lady isn't married?'

My thoughts were interrupted when I heard the sound of high heels clicking down the hallway coming from the operating room, and, as if she could read my mind, I would soon know the answer to the question I had just asked myself.

The clicking stopped. I heard a gentle rap on my office door. I always left the door partially open. Looking up, I saw Martha Hall peeking around the door. 'My God,' I thought, 'she's even beautiful in curlers!'

"Hello-ooo. It's too early to go to sleep … can we talk?"

I always kept a swivel chair next to my desk for visitors and students. I waved my hand at it and said, "Please do."

"I hear you work for Western Electric."

"I do."

"What do you do here?"

"I hire and train people to install telephone equipment. Western Electric manufactures the equipment and we also install it. I'm with the installation organization. Your company and mine are separate companies but we are both subsidiaries of AT&T. At the present time I head up the Detroit Installation Areas Hiring and Training program for Western Electric."

"One of the operators just told me you were married."

Oh! Oh! I felt as if someone had just stuck a dagger in my heart and this dream was going to soon end. Everyone here knew that I was married, but evidently everyone did not know that I was getting a divorce. Defensively, I responded,

"Yes, but you have to emphasize the word '*were*.' I'm going through a divorce right now, but it's not something I like to talk about." Back in those days there was no such thing as 'No Fault,' and it took a long time to get a divorce.

"Do you have children?"

Now the dagger had just been twisted.

"Two teenage boys."

I didn't think anyone knew that! I expected the axe to really fall now, and I lamely launched into an explanation.

"My wife plans to marry some guy as soon as our divorce is final. In the meantime, we're separated and the boys are living with her. It's a long story. They live in Warren and I live by myself in an apartment in Madison Heights."

I thought … 'This is it' … until I heard her response.

"Well … *I am* divorced … and, as you know, have

a daughter. Are we still going skiing this weekend?"
'Wow, could this day get any better?' I wondered.
    "As far as I'm concerned, it's in the bank," I said.

After Martha left, I wondered if I had a 'tiger by the tail.' But as I pondered, I thought that it could be a *good* thing for me at this time of my life. Tiger or not, though, all I knew is that I was in love. This could be the best thing that ever happened to me and I certainly did not want to blow it.

During the night it had stopped snowing and Gratiot Avenue had been plowed. Most of the schools had reopened and public transportation was back in business. My students showed up for class in the morning, and for me it was a very long day. I did see Martha Hall briefly. We exchanged phone numbers and she suggested that I call her that night so we could make plans for our ski date.

    With little sleep the past night I was really tired. I also needed to clean up, but first I went to dinner at that new steak house. It was great, and a place I thought I would like to go back to.

    Once home I shaved, showered and changed into clean jeans and a T- shirt. I intended to call Martha at nine, and since I kept my phone on the kitchen table, I found myself sitting there staring at it long before nine. Nervously drumming my fingers on the table in anticipation of hearing her voice again, I could see her image in my head as I waited.

    About 5'6" tall, and around 115 pounds, Martha had a body that some women would kill for. I thought that she was not only beautiful, but her every movement radiated class. At the same time a line from "Some Enchanted Evening," from the musical *South Pacific* was running through my head over and over again: *"Once you have found her, never let her go!"*

I felt like I had to go through with this ski thing now no matter what the consequences were. Having lied was bad enough, but confessing now was absolutely out of the question. And, who knows ... she might be a beginner herself. I liked that thought, and decided not to worry about it. Just let the chips fall where they may and hope for best.

Sitting there at the table watching the big hand on my watch slowly creeping toward nine, I felt my anxiety mounting by the minute. It was like waiting for water to boil. And it seemed like an eternity, but the big hand was finally pointing to nine, so I picked up the phone and nervously dialed her number.

Fortunately, she answered on the first ring. The sound of her voice completely relieved my anxiety. I wondered, 'Did she answer so quickly because she didn't want her daughter to wake up?' Or was she waiting by the phone for the same reason I was?

"Can you talk?" I asked.

"Sure, Dianne's sleeping."

My heartbeat slowed and I relaxed as we made arrangements to ski Pine Knob on Sunday.

"I'm going to leave Dianne with her grandparents Friday night for the weekend and I'll pick her up Monday after work." At least I knew her daughter's name now.

"Dianne's grandparents live in Royal Oak, about ten minutes from my apartment. That way we have the whole weekend if you want. I was planning on going to Eastland Saturday to pick up a few things I'll need Sunday. Why don't you come along? Don't you need anything, like … maybe ski gloves or something? We could have lunch in the Mall, go to a movie if you like, or … come back to my place." I really liked the "come back to my place!"

"Sounds great to me," I said. All she had to do was ask, and I would have gone anywhere with her. But now I had to find out what I might need for the weekend.

After I hung up I dialed Rex, a former neighbor who I knew was a skier. Knowing Rex, I was sure he would still be up. After he answered, and I explained my predicament, he said, "Well, you picked the right place all right. Pine Knob's not much of a hill, but it's great for beginners. They make their own snow there, weather permitting. If it's cold wear long underwear and jeans. I know you have a winter jacket, driving gloves will work, and I think a baseball cap will do, so all you should have to do is rent the ski equipment. Their attendants are pretty good at Pine Knob, that's all they do all day … don't worry, they'll fit you up with everything you'll need. And if I were you, I would stick to the rope tow and bunny hill … snow plowing."

"Snow plowing?" I asked

He laughed and said, "The first thing you have to learn is how to stop, that's very important. Just look around at the other beginners and you'll know what

I mean."

"So I've got everything I need?"

"For this weekend you have, but if she's a good skier, and you want to ski with her again, you're going to have to get some equipment and a ski outfit of your own. And it might be a good idea if you took some lessons. Good luck old buddy, hope it works out for you. Let me know, OK?"

"You bet ... and I absolutely have to make this thing work."

CHAPTER THREE

MARTHA'S APARTMENT WAS ON THE CORNER OF THIRTEEN MILE ROAD AND CROOKS ROAD, in Royal Oak … less than ten minutes west of mine. It was on the second floor of a family-friendly complex, and consisted of two tiny bedrooms, a small bathroom, a kitchen—barely large enough for one cook—and a combination living/dining room.

I picked her up at nine-thirty and we were in Eastland Mall by ten, just as it opened. We spent the morning shopping, had lunch at J. L. Hudson's at twelve, couldn't find a movie we wanted to see, and so we were back at her place by two.

Martha made a pot of coffee and we sat in her living room talking for hours. I found out that she was born in Detroit, was twenty-eight and had graduated from Cooley High School on the west side. She had gone to Wayne State University on a scholarship … hated to cook (I loved to) … she did not like liver (neither did I) … and her maiden name was Ziets.

She had grown up in a blue-collar neighborhood in a very modest house. Her father, Julius, whom everyone called 'Duke,' was a housepainter. She had a stepmother named Eva and two older brothers, Alfred and Arthur, and a younger sister, Helen.

I learned later that Martha's mother had been born in Prague, Czechoslovakia, now called the Czech

Republic. Her mother had apparently abandoned the family shortly after Helen's birth and was never heard from again.

Like me, Martha didn't like to talk about her prior marriage or the details of her divorce. She did say that Dianne had been born in Chicago and, despite the divorce, she was on good terms with Dianne's grandparents.

At about ten o'clock I got up the nerve to put my arm around her, gave her a hug, kissed her on her cheek as I left, then, reluctantly, went home.

The next morning couldn't come soon enough. As I tossed and turned, I experienced an almost psychotic range of emotions. On one hand, I was thrilled to be going on this date; on the other, I knew that I was about to be exposed and feared the consequences when Martha found out that I had never set foot on a ski slope before. Despite the almost sleepless night, in the morning I put the best possible face on, and picked her up for the drive to Pine Knob.

Pine Knob is a small ski area in Clarkston, Michigan, near Detroit. Things went just as Rex had said. Returning to my car we put the rental gear on. Then we clattered across the parking lot to the bunny hill and rope tow. This wasn't easy. I noticed that other people put their boots on in the locker room and then *carried* their skis and poles over to the rope tow, thus eliminating having to clatter across the parking lot in their skis as we did; we were doing it the hard way. (Rex didn't tell me about this part.) I turned to Martha and said,

"You know, I think we just did this thing wrong.

I think we should have put our boots on in the locker room and our skis on at the bunny hill."

"I think you're right … why didn't you say something?"

"You got me there; I thought *you* were a skier."

"If you recall, I asked *you* if *you* were a skier, and *you* said you were. I, on the other hand, **never** said '*I*' was."

"But if I had said I *wasn't*, would we be here today?" She smiled, reached over and gave me a peck on the cheek, saying,

"I *know* we would. You had nothing to fear."

After a very short day of tough, beginner 'snow plowing,' we tired, and decided to have an early dinner. We stopped at the Fox and Hounds restaurant on Woodward Avenue. The dinner was great and we lingered over two glasses of fine wine just talking. When I took her home she asked if I wanted to come in. And that was just what I hoped she would say. Much, much later … when I left her apartment, this time the kiss was not on her cheek, and I was walking on air. I could hardly wait to call Rex. When I did he seemed delighted.

"Do you think that you'll be skiing with her again?"

"I would bet on it,"

"I'm really happy for you Bob, and I know Jan [Rex's wife] will be too. I hope you guys like skiing as much as we do. And good luck with that lady. What's her name?"

"Martha."

Soon after our little ski trip we were going steady. We discussed the fact that my divorce hadn't gone through yet and Martha said she didn't mind what others thought; it was none of their business.

In the beginning, we often stopped at a local bar for a glass of wine on our way home. Then, Martha would pick Dianne up at her grandmother's house while I went somewhere for dinner alone and then on to my apartment.

When we tired of that and wanted to spend more time together, I would pick up Chinese, Kentucky Fried Chicken or pizza on my way home, and the three of us would eat at her place.

Dianne and I hit it off the first time I met her. She was adorable, as cute as a button, a bright lovable chatterbox, but pleasantly so. Fortunately, she didn't seem at all disturbed by the fact that she had to share her mother with me. In fact, it wasn't long before Dianne and I were going on adventures of our own. In those days I was an avid fisherman and would sometimes cast for bass late at night on nearby Loon Lake. Dianne expressed an interest in my fishing, so I asked her if she wanted to row the boat while I did my casting on those trips. She readily agreed and I found her to be a delightful and charming companion. I believe that our fishing trips were the beginning of a loving relationship that we share to this day.

I also taught her how to play chess, but quit playing after several months when she consistently started to beat me.

When the movie *The Sound of Music* came out, we saw it five or six times. We probably would have seen it more, but Martha diplomatically said that, although she really liked it, she had had enough. So did I, but I thought it better if Martha said it.

Martha encouraged my relationship with Dianne and invited me to join them in Tobermory, Ontario, where Dianne was spending the summer at her grandparents' cottage. By this time I had met her grandparents, the Halls, and, although it was a four-hour drive, I was delighted that she asked me. Trying to read between the lines, I saw this invitation as something very special.

Tobermory is a small fishing village located at the tip of the Bruce Peninsula in Ontario, Canada. The Bruce peninsula is a finger of land that separates Lake Huron from Georgian Bay and is, geologically, part of the Niagara Escarpment. The scenery is truly spectacular with towering cliffs and limestone formations very similar to the Pictured Rocks National Lakeshore in Michigan's Upper Peninsula. This particular summer, work had just been completed on the Bruce Trail, beginning in Niagara Falls and terminating in Tobermory, 885 kilometers away.

Once in Tobermory, I checked into the motel I had reserved for the occasion (actually the only one in town), and then, following Martha's instructions, drove the short distance to the Halls' cottage in the woods.

When I arrived at the cottage I found the main topic of conversation was the recent completion of the Bruce Trail and the fact that the last leg of the trail, which ended in Tobermory, was on the face of the cliff behind the Hall property. Mrs. Hall mentioned that there was a path leading to the trail in the rear of their lot.

I think it was Dianne who asked how far the trail was from their lot to Tobermory. Her grandmother said, "Let's see … we've never been on the trail, but it's almost three miles by road, and it would be somewhat less by the trail."

There was no doubt in my mind that Dianne was gung-ho about taking that trail to Tobermory. Martha said, "Let's do it, but it would have to be tomorrow." She thought that it was too late to try it that day. I don't think Dianne got much sleep that night.

Since I thought this was going to be a walk in the park, I arrived the next day with my Nikon around my neck, and when we started out it didn't look very bad … but about one mile in, it started to get more difficult … and the next mile was downright treacherous. In fact, had I known the risk involved, I *never* would have agreed to take that hike.

We soon found out that we were now on the side of a towering cliff with the ice cold water of Georgian Bay crashing on the stone walls far below us. Also, that part of the trail meandered in and out of the various bays and inlets that make up the Niagara Escarpment. In many places one misstep meant certain death.

I was in the lead, and when I came to a two-foot gap in the trail we had to traverse, I hesitated and thought of our options. There were only two. One was to go back, but I immediately ruled that out thinking that we had come too far and it would just be too dangerous to turn back. At the same time I had no idea what lay ahead, but I did see a trail marker on the face of the cliff and hoped that we were nearing the end, so I traversed the gap. Turning around, I extended my hand to Dianne and then to Martha, helping them to cross. It was just plain luck, but I had made the right decision; the trail improved and we were soon in a Tobermory ice cream parlor buying cones for the long walk home.

Looking back all these years now, and Dianne agrees with me, that trip and hike created a bond which served to cement a relationship between the three of us that would last for the rest of our lives. And, I believe that it was soon assumed by most everyone that Martha and I were more than "just friends." It also was the beginning of a friendship between me and the Halls that has lasted a lifetime.

CHAPTER FOUR

O F COURSE, ALL OF THIS TRAVELING AND DATING DID NOT GO UNNOTICED AT THE OFFICE. In between classes one day, while I was going over the results of a recent test, my phone rang. It was one of the other Group Chief Operators that I had known for years. In fact, we had had lunch together one Saturday at Eastland shortly before I met Martha. She said that she heard I was dating Miss Hall and wanted to know if it was true. I told her it was, and she said,

"Oh … I could never compete with Miss Hall!"

I thought that was strange, I had only had lunch with this lady once, but she must have read something into that lunch that got past me. And she must have known about my pending divorce. I knew that certain people at WECO were aware of it, but I surmised that people at MBT were not. But I later found that I was wrong.

I should have known better. Most of my peers knew about it and due to the nature of our business they all worked in telephone offices. So it should have occurred to me that gossip like that travels fast. Then, after all the times I had worked in operating rooms, I was a fool to think I could keep such a secret.

I recall an incident when I was a young supervisor with men working in this same operating room. The Chief asked to speak to me in her office. She then asked me if one particular worker of mine was married. There was no way I would lie for this guy and I told her that he was. She then said that the man was dating one of her girls and had told her he was *not* married. Things were very different back then. Some Chief Operators were more like "mother hens" and those operators out there were like family. She put an end to that romance right then and there by asking me to transfer that man to another location, preferably out of the building. Much to his chagrin, my employee was gone the next morning.

Shortly after that somewhat perplexing call, I answered my phone, and found my boss on the line. There was a lull in hiring and he asked,

"You don't have much going on for awhile do you?"

"Not much … things have been pretty slow lately," I answered.

"Have you ever been to Iron Mountain?"

"If you mean the Iron Mountain in the Upper Peninsula … no."

"Well, they just hired ten people up there and they would like you to come up and teach a class. I would appreciate it if you can squeeze it in."

"When?" I asked.

"How about a week from Monday, can you do that?"

"If they can help me out with a few things I'll need, sure."

What else could I say? I really didn't want to go to Iron Mountain at this time of my life, but I saw no way out of it. Iron Mountain is a long way from

Detroit … and, most importantly, a long way from Martha.

By then most everyone in the office knew about my divorce and that I was going with Martha, and if I had to describe our relationship at that particular time I would refer you to the lyrics of the song "Fever."

We would have to cancel plans we had made for that week, but I could see no way out of it. Martha was disappointed, but she understood. She did ask me if I would spend Friday evening with her, and leave from her place. I should have thought of the problem this would mean, but I was in love and wild horses couldn't have stopped me anyway!

Friday afternoon I rented a station wagon, picked up everything I needed from the telephone office, showered at my apartment and went to Martha's. We were lovers now, and after a very romantic evening I was on my way at about ten o'clock … much too late … I had stayed too long.

The bridge between Mackinaw City in the Lower Peninsula and St. Ignace, in the Upper Peninsula, is one of the world's longest suspension bridges. I don't remember what time it was when I crossed that bridge, but I do know I was fighting to stay awake, and still had a long way to go. So I turned the radio up, opened the windows and started to sing. Then, soon after I left St. Ignace, things really got bad; it started to snow. I was on a two-lane highway with no street lights and the snow was blowing straight at me, making it very difficult to see. I have never driven a car in such conditions before, or since. I was extremely lucky to have made it at all.

I don't know how I did it, but somehow I rolled into Iron Mountain at dawn, found my motel, checked in at the desk, went to my room, plopped on the bed fully clothed and was just about to crash when the phone rang. My first thought was that it was the desk, but only I knew where I was staying. But it was Martha; she wanted to know if I was all right.

"I'm fine," I said. "I just got here and am about to pass out. I'll call you later, when I wake up, Sweetie."

As I hung up I wondered how she knew where I was staying. I couldn't recall telling her. But then, I knew that she had graduated with honors, didn't I?

I knew Iron Mountain bordered Wisconsin, but I did not know that it was only 90 miles from Green Bay, the home of the Green Bay Packers. Or that it was noted for having the Pine Mountain Ski Jump there … one of the world's highest ski jumps. Skiers came from all over the world to jump there.

In my spare time I used to hang out in a coffee shop where I became friends with the owner. Behind the counter there were pictures all over the wall of an Olympic skier jumping from Pine Mountain. When I asked him about the pictures he said that he was the skier.

He was once an Olympic jumper. He said that the Pine Mountain Jump was only a short distance from his shop, so I went out to look at it. I found that halfway down the jump there was an observation deck. I went down there and when I looked up at where they jumped from, and where they landed, I couldn't believe how anyone had the guts to do such a thing.

Back at his shop I asked him how they could do it. He said, "Well, when I was about three years old I would jump from a two-foot hill. And for the next sixteen years I kept increasing the size of the hills."

Iron Mountain is one of the many great tourist areas in what we Michiganders call the "UP." Needless to say, though, I was glad to return to my true love when the week was over. Only, on my return, I took my sweet time about it. I was wide awake and felt that it was much safer that way.

CHAPTER FIVE

IT WASN'T LONG AFTER I RETURNED that my brother Glen and his wife Barbara joined us on some dates and even ski trips. They also lived in Royal Oak near Crooks Road, coincidently within walking distance from Martha's apartment.

My divorce was finally settled and I was a free man by then, so we soon became a foursome on many occasions, especially skiing. Brother Glen and I were always very close; we were able to visit with each other many times while in the service. Before he went overseas we were able to meet in Chicago, Huston, and Lincoln, Nebraska. Then, after he came back from England, he once flew a training mission with me in Ardmore, Oklahoma, just before *I* went overseas. On the cover of the *"Blues"* is a picture of Glen and me standing beside the aircraft we were about to board for that 'mission.'

We did all of our skiing in Michigan in those days. By then we had our own gear and proper ski wear, had taken some lessons and were parallel skiing. We skied Caberfae, near Cadillac; Boyne Mountain, near Boyne Falls; and Boyne Highlands, near Harbor Springs. We had many good times together. Martha fit in with my side of the family like a glove.

This went on for almost two wonderful years. On the fourth of July in 1966 we celebrated by making two toasts, one for Independence Day, and another because Martha had just made a landmark promotion the day before. She was now a 'Chief Operator.'

In all my life I have never met anyone like her. As far as I was concerned there just *wasn't* anyone else like her. To me she was everything I wanted in a woman, and then some. So it was no surprise to anyone when we announced that we were going to get married. We set the date for September 29, 1967.

WECO's hiring program had dried up and I was now back in the field working jobs in the main Bell building in downtown Detroit at 1365 Cass Avenue. On July 23, 1967, one of the worst riots in American history broke out, and I found myself working practically in the middle of it.

Most people believe that the riot was triggered by an overly aggressive police raid on an afterhours drinking club, or "blind pig," in a black neighborhood on the Northwest side. Within 48 hours of the raid, looting, vandalism and fires spread throughout Northwest Detroit and then into the East side.

Governor George Romney mobilized the National Guard immediately. When the riot spread to the East side, President Lyndon Johnson ordered the U.S. Army's 82nd Airborne to Detroit.

Most Western Electric management people were also top-notch skilled testers and could be used to restore telephone service in case of emergency service interruptions. These men had been screened by the FBI and carried identification cards that allowed them to enter any telephone office in the USA during national emergencies.

This was a national emergency, and I was one of those people that carried one of those identification cards. So I was expected to be at 1365 Cass Avenue every day of the riot in case of an equipment failure. I had to drive 12 miles down Woodward Avenue, sometimes behind Army tanks or troop carriers, through thick smoke, passing burning buildings and fire trucks, with snipers shooting at us from the open windows of nearby buildings.

Just inside the 20-story building, before I reached the elevators, I had to pass about 20 U.S. soldiers armed with rifles with fixed bayonets guarding the main lobby. Once safely inside, telephone company switchmen—and WECO management people— spent most of our time in the cafeteria on the 19th floor drinking coffee and watching the fires scattered all over the city below.

Order was finally restored on July 27, 1967. In the five days of rioting, 43 people had been killed and 1,189 were injured. More than 7,000 people were arrested and 2,000 buildings were destroyed. Fortunately, Martha's office was in no danger of the riot.

Exactly two months and two days later, on September 29, 1967, six people gathered in the courtroom of the Municipal Judge in the City Hall of Royal Oak, Michigan. Neither Martha nor I wanted a big wedding. Brother Glen and his wife Barbara were there as witnesses. Martha's father, Duke, whom I knew loved his daughter dearly, and was very proud of her, sat alone in the front row.

Martha was absolutely stunning. When we left the

courtroom, we were Mr. and Mrs. Robert Thornton and my dream had finally come true. Martha was 31 and I was 42, and I thought I was the luckiest guy in the world. And from that day on, Martha became the most precious thing in my life, not that she hadn't been since we met, but now it was '*till death do us part.*'

We spent a wonderful delayed honeymoon in Michigan's beautiful Upper Peninsula. We picked the first week in October, usually the best week of the year for color. The vivid reds, yellows, oranges and greens are a photographer's paradise.

We visited Mackinac Island, saw the beautiful upper and lower Tahquamenon Falls. Munising, with its Pictured Rocks, Copper Harbor in the Keweenaw Peninsula, Iron Mountain, Ironwood, next door to Hurly, Wisconsin with all of its bars, Lake of the Clouds in the Porcupine Mountains, Bond Falls … just to name a few of the spectacular places in the UP.

I have always been, and still am, a rabid fan of the University of Michigan's football team … go blue!

We were on our way home from our honeymoon on the Saturday that Michigan was playing their arch rival Ohio State. We were somewhere in upper Michigan and had plenty of time … after all, the next day was Sunday. So I asked Martha if she would mind if we stopped at a motel so we could see the game on television.

Martha said that she didn't mind and agreed. So we stopped at the next motel, rented a room, watched the game, and left.

I have often wondered what the motel clerk thought when we left without staying the night. Anyway, we drove until sundown, stopped at another hotel for the night and returned home the next morning.

CHAPTER SIX

DURING THE LAST ICE AGE, a glacier, like a giant bulldozer coming out of what is now Canada, leveled the Detroit area as it moved south. Then, 20,000 years ago, it stopped and melted, leaving an irregular line where most everything south of where it melted was as flat as a pancake and everything north of it was undisturbed.

Consequently, the area north of Twenty-eight Mile Road is rolling hills and fresh water lakes, whereas the Detroit area is flat. Since then those rolling hills have become a paradise, creating places like Bloomfield Hills, Rochester, Birmingham, Franklin Hills and the village of Romeo, just to name a few. On the very edge of those hills, four miles south of the village of Romeo, lies the small town of Washington, in Washington Township.

After the wedding, I moved in with Martha and Dianne in Martha's tiny apartment on Thirteen Mile Road. Martha and I had planned on buying a home of our own after we got married so we started hunting for something immediately.

Martha had not done so before I met her because, in those days, it was extremely difficult for a woman, especially a single woman, to obtain credit. Despite the success or stability in a woman's employment history, lenders viewed their employment as a temporary condition subject to termination upon marriage or pregnancy.

Creditors required women to find male co-signers, discounted their income or placed other roadblocks in their path when they tried to secure credit. This non-economic gender-based discrimination was finally addressed by Congress in 1976 in the Equal Credit Opportunity Act. Fortunately, being that I was a male with an established credit history at that time, we had no problem.

Martha agreed with me on new construction, so we began our search. We looked for something we liked and could afford, and finally signed a contract with a builder to construct a 2,800 square foot three-level house with an octagon shaped living room and two fireplaces—one in the family room and one in the living room.

It was on a two-acre lot on the very top of a hill in a cul-de-sac called 'Fox Point' in the brand new bedroom community of Carriage Hills, about two miles west of Washington, Michigan.

Carriage Hills was surrounded by a state park, apple orchards, peach orchards and farms. It was only about four miles south of Romeo. We agreed to pay the builder $40,000.00 for the two-acre lot and house. Martha was delighted. I had never seen her happier. This pleased me very much.

Martha's father Duke was a retired painter by trade. So we worked out a deal with the builder to knock $1,000 off the price of the house if we painted the inside. ($1,000 in those days was a lot of money.) And we did. We worked every weekend until the inside was finished. Duke, Martha, Dianne and I worked until we dropped. But we were very happy with the house when it was finished.

We moved in, in 1968, and found that on a clear night we could see a faint halo of lights over Detroit from the balcony of our master bedroom 28 miles away.

Landscaping was not included in the price of the house, but grading around the house was. So with the help of Martha, Dianne and some friends and neighbors, we laid the sod and landscaped the graded areas around the house. We then purchased a John Deere riding mower with a detachable trailer and snow blower. It had three blades with a 42-inch cut. I had a shed built in the very back end of the property for the John Deere and other landscaping equipment.

The back yard was at least 50 feet below the house, sitting on top of the hill. Because of erosion,

I had about 50 railroad ties brought in, and with Dianne's help we terraced off the hill together, and planted spreaders on every level. This was not easy and took several months to accomplish. But it took care of the erosion problem and provided a wonderful view of the house from the rear of the lot.

I knew Martha did not like cooking and later I found out that she did not like shopping in supermarkets very much either. But I soon learned that although she liked the fact that I did the cooking, she always set the table and helped clean up the mess after dinner. Even when it came to cleaning pots and pans, we always did it together until it was done. Before I retired we also shared the housekeeping chores on weekends. As far as supermarket shopping went, I always believed that the cook had to do that anyway. I soon found out neither Martha nor Dianne had an aversion to manual labor. They both pitched in without an argument whenever necessary.

It wasn't very long after we moved in, a few months perhaps, when I overheard an event that, looking back on it today, I believe was probably one of the many things that made our marriage so harmonious. I happened to be in the family room one day when I overheard Martha and Dianne having an argument in the kitchen. I don't remember what they *were* arguing about, but they were arguing. Then, suddenly, within seconds, they were talking like old friends again.

Now, if that had been my father and mother, or my ex and me, that argument might have gone on for weeks, with lots of hard feelings and long silent spells in between. I thought, 'What a difference!' I can honestly say (although no one believes me) that I cannot recall Martha and me *ever* having a *serious* argument, and the *few times* we might have even come close to one, it was quickly forgotten and out of the way before it could go anywhere. We were actually living by the old axiom: *don't sweat the small stuff, and most everything's small stuff.* I knew that I had married a very unique and unusual woman, but, little by little, I was finding out just *how unusually unique she really was.*

Dianne was going to school in Romeo now, and we found the area a wonderful place to live. Our social life, which wasn't much in those days, was centered in Romeo. The historic village of Romeo is famous for its orchards and annual peach festival. The village had a population of about 3,600 in those days and I believe it hasn't changed much to this day, with all the growth being outside of the village. I was still with Western Electric but was now working out of an office in the nearby city of Mount Clemens.

In 1969 Martha suggested that we put in a Gunite swimming pool in the back yard near the base of the hill. After deciding on a contractor we agreed on a 20x40 kidney-shaped pool about 200 feet from the house. When finished, it held 37,000 gallons of water. At the deep end it was six feet deep and included a diving board. A cement deck and a three-foot wrought iron fence surrounded the pool with a latch gate at the shallow end facing the house.

A water line was installed from the pool to a few feet from the kitchen door so the pool could be filled easily from just outside the house. The first time we viewed the beautifully landscaped pool below us from the top of the hill, and I saw the happy look on my wife's face, I just couldn't resist the temptation to pull her close and give her a big kiss.

The last time we saw this pool was in 2002, and the pool looked like it was brand new. The same family owned the house who bought it from us in 1983, and they have done a wonderful job in keeping up the property.

In 1969 we also acquired a 60-pound Black Labrador we named Miss-T and adopted a 15-pound black Poodle we named Gypsy. This would be our home for over 15 wonderful years.

Every telephone office had huge power plants and generators. The generators could supply enough power to keep the office working as long as they had the fuel to operate them. Although we did not install the generators, we did install the power plants and the many fluorescent lights and switches, as well as power outlets that went into a telephone office in those days.

Because of my many experiences working on every facet of a telephone office, I was able to finish off several basements in houses I owned. So my next major project at Fox Point was to finish off the basement.

I was really into amateur photography in those days so I wanted a place to show my many slides. After doing all of the electrical stuff required I installed both wall and floor cabinets and a sink and counter space to accommodate my camera equipment, which included a projector.

Then I constructed all the walls on the floor and Martha helped me hoist them up while I nailed them to the rafters and floor. On the far wall, hiding the furnace, hot water tank and my work bench, I installed dry wall and a door.

I filled the side walls with insulation and finished them with wood paneling. I then painted the far wall ceiling white, so I was able to project a picture on that wall in about a six foot square. We then had professionals install carpeting on the stairs and floor to finish it off. This room really came in handy for showing slides to friends and family, as well as to my softball team each year at the end of the season.

CHAPTER SEVEN

THE VILLAGE OF ROMEO WAS FOUNDED IN 1830 and has never had a major fire. Consequently, there are many historical homes and buildings in the village that go back as far as the Civil War. In fact, every year the citizens of Romeo hold an historical home walk, a day when people living in historical homes open them to the public. At one time, the village was considered for the site of the University of Michigan, but Ann Arbor beat them out.

One Sunday morning, over coffee, Martha read in the local newspaper that there was an historical building in downtown Romeo for sale. She thought that it might be a good investment. We investigated and found it to be over one hundred years old. It was a two-story brick building in excellent shape located on Main Street. A French restaurant leased the first floor and a beauty parlor the second. We thought the price was right and we bought it. (Several years later we sold it and made a handsome profit.)

About one year later, in the middle of the night, the phone rang. Bleary eyed, I looked at the electric clock on the vanity on my side of the bed. Ye gods … it was two in the morning!

"It's for you," this sweet, sexy, sleepy voice said coming from the other side of the bed. The phone was on her side.

"Who would be calling at this hour?"

"Some State Trooper," she said as she tossed the receiver to my side of the bed, dismissing the subject since the call was not for her. I grabbed the phone and said,

"Hey!"

"It's Tom, Bob. You better get up here. Your front door is wide open, all the lights are on, mashed potatoes are on the wall and a ring is on one of the tables." He was obviously talking about the French restaurant.

"Be there in ten minutes Tom, thanks."

When I got to the restaurant it looked like Tom and his partner were standing guard. Both troopers played on my slow-pitch softball team. I was a playing manager and one of the founders of a thirty-five-and-over softball league. My team was called 'The Ugly Mugs,' named after 'The Ugly Mug Restaurant and Bar' on Main Street, owned by a friend of mine who sponsored the team.

"Hi guys. Looks like John and Michelle (the leaseholders of the restaurant) had a little spat," I said as I picked up Michelle's wedding ring from one of the tables.

"Thanks again for calling. I'll lock up and get it cleaned up in the morning."

When I got home Martha was awake and sitting up in bed. Curiosity got the best of her as I silently undressed … and she finally said,

"Okay Robert, what happened?"

When talking to me she always called me Robert, when talking *about me*, she called me Bob.

"Not much," I said as I went to her side of the bed, bent down and kissed her on that cute little nose looking up at me.

"John and Michelle must have had an argument, messed up the place, and left the door wide open. Take care of this in case Michelle wants it back," I said, as I gave her Michelle's ring. "I'll make sure John cleans the place up in the morning."

Then I snuggled up with her and tried my best to go back to sleep.

In those days Martha and I were smokers. When I was in the service I never smoked. In fact, we were issued two cartons of cigarettes each month, but I never had a problem selling mine for as much as five dollars. In those days five dollars was a lot of money.

Years later, while working for Western Electric, I started smoking. I tried many times to quit, but it wasn't until the late seventies that I succeeded. Then I spent the next four or five years trying to get Martha to quit. I never will forget my driving someplace with Martha and she would light up a cigarette. So when Martha lit up, I would push the button and open her window. The problem with that was she could close it. So we would be driving along with her window going, up and down, up and down, until she put the cigarette out. She never said anything, and she never appeared to get angry. In fact, I believe she found it amusing. But she never quit until she was a vice president of Ameritech in Chicago, and the Chairman of the Board banned smoking in the building.

CHAPTER EIGHT

M Y NEXT DOOR NEIGHBOR WAS A ROTARIAN and he talked me into joining the club. It was a good move. Now I was able to make friends with most of the orchard owners, farmers and business men in the area.

It was then that I learned a lot about growing fruit. For example, I never knew there were so many varieties of apples and peaches. And along with insects, worms, etc., one of their biggest enemies was hail. Hail could ruin a crop rather quickly … especially peaches.

I also met other prominent people, some who later played on my softball team. Besides the two state troopers, I had two well-known lawyers and our district judge, called by some 'the hanging judge,' on our team. I believe he was called the hanging judge because he was known to go by the book, and gave no quarter, no matter who the accused or their lawyers might be.

We had slowly developed a large circle of friends by now and our social life had increased dramatically. One of my best friends was the Bruce Township Supervisor. Martha and I became personal friends with all of the restaurant owners in Romeo and most of the business people. I was one of the charter members of the Veterans of Foreign Wars (VFW) club when it was first established in Romeo.

Mickey Lolich, the Hall of Fame pitcher for the Detroit Tigers, lived about one hundred yards from our house. Mickey is the *only* pitcher in baseball history to win three games in one World Series. And he did it while he was our neighbor.

I played many positions on my softball team over the years, but when I played shortstop or third base, whenever we made double plays it was Thornton to Thornton to Thornton. My brother Wayne played second base, and my oldest son, Tom, then 35, played first base.

At the end of every season we had a family and team bash at our house to celebrate the past season. I could always count on getting thrown into the pool, so I learned to take my wallet out of my jeans before the festivities began. They didn't care if I was wearing street clothes or not.

That's when the room in the basement came in handy. We had a few folding chairs and were able to borrow enough to seat the whole gang. During the season I had taken many slides of our games, and when shown properly they could be rather amusing.

The judge made a very good master of ceremonies and always made a hilarious speech before the slide show. His speech always included inexpensive amusing prizes for some players. He once gave my brother Wayne a burnt-out light bulb wrapped in Christmas tissue. The following year Wayne presented the judge with a hangman's noose he made very cleverly out of matchsticks and glue.

Years later, when I went to say goodbye to the

judge in his chambers before Martha and I left for Chicago, I noticed that hangman's noose prominently displayed on his desk. He was obviously very proud of it.

After we moved to Chicago, whenever we visited family in Michigan, we always included our friends in Romeo. The last time we were there, one of our ex-neighbors held a party for us. Practically the whole softball team was there and the judge was the last one to arrive. When he did, he stopped the festivities, called everyone around him, pulled my old jersey out of a bag, and proceeded to make a speech declaring my jersey officially retired. Martha had secretly provided him with the jersey, which I still have to this day.

We always had one heck of a time getting in and out of Carriage Hills when it snowed. The roads were all hills and curves so Martha bought an Oldsmobile Tornado. It was the first front wheel-drive in the neighborhood. Martha was always the first one out in the morning. She was an early bird and her office was in downtown Detroit—a long commute.

Because we lived on a cul-de-sac, on all the bad snowy days the business men on the street used to sit around their living room windows enjoying a cup of hot coffee waiting to see if Martha was going to get out and blaze a trail for them. We found that those new front wheel-drives were amazing. And, if my memory serves me correctly, she might have been the only one at times, but she always made it out. Nothing stopped her determination to get to work.

One day Martha came home from work and said that someone had given her two tickets to the Michigan/ Notre Dame Football game which, was being played in Ann Arbor the next week. We were delighted.

When we arrived at the stadium we found that we were sitting in the student section. Michigan's football stadium could seat over one hundred thousand fans. I thought it was rather amusing when they started passing young ladies up from the bottom of the stadium to the top. Even, later, during the game, I didn't mind inhaling all of the strange second-hand smoke around us. In fact, I felt rather good about it. I whispered to Martha,

"What kind of cigarettes are they smoking? What a strange smelling smoke." She looked at me, laughed, and with a smile whispered back …

"Marijuana, you doe-doe."

Then I realized I was getting high on second-hand smoke. That could explain why it didn't matter so much to me when Michigan lost to Notre Dame 7 to 6. This was my first and last experience with marijuana, and I can truthfully say I never smoked it. But, unlike one of our presidents, I can't say I never inhaled it.

Although I had played golf before, it was when I lived in Carriage Hills that I took it up seriously. There were many courses nearby, and my restaurant friend and I joined a group of golfers who played on all of them. One of our golfers owned an RV lot, so at times we would all take a golf trip to places like Kalamazoo, Grand Rapids and other towns with great courses. That was also when Martha first took up the game on weekends, and she fell in love with it.

In 1973 Western Electric sent me to New York City on a temporary transfer. They put me up in an apartment at 52nd and 3rd, in Manhattan. I was within walking distance of the United Nations, Rockefeller Center, Grand Circus Park and great museums. WECO would fly me home and back on weekends, or would fly Martha to New York and back.

Since she had never been to New York before she opted for the Big Apple the very first weekend. We fell in love with Broadway, the wonderful restaurants and Grand Circus Park. We saw *Cats*, *The Phantom of the Opera*, *Fiddler on the Roof*, *Les Misérables* and many other great shows.

We loved the great restaurants … Tavern on the Green, Sardis and the Rainbow Room were just some of our favorite restaurants. Grand Circus Park itself is enough to make one want to come back to this marvelous city. We had such a good time, Martha came back every weekend and I never got back to Carriage Hills until my job was done in New York. We liked the city so much we returned to visit it for many years.

CHAPTER NINE

IN 1976 WESTERN ELECTRIC WAS FACING VERY SERIOUS PROBLEMS. I had been through many bad times before, but this time it was different. The future telephone equipment was obviously going to be a solid state computerized switching system we called ESS, for 'Electronic Switching Systems.'

I knew very little about the ESS system. Until now everything was electromagnetic and I had built a career on it. I had 30 years' service with the company at the time and could see the handwriting on the wall. Soon my services would no longer be required. Technology was going to put me out of business. So when I was offered a retirement package I could not refuse; I took it.

For many years I had worked very closely with the MBT's engineers and the WECO-owned Bell Labs. When I retired, the MBT engineering department offered me a job to work for them as an engineering consultant. I took that job for almost two years, and when the assignment I was working on was complete they offered me another.

But at that particular time things at home were getting rather strained. Martha was stretching herself thin with her long commute and added responsibilities. However, she never once complained and I am sure she didn't let it affect her work, but there was now a way we could act to make things much easier on both of us.

I was always the full-time chief cook and bottle washer, plus the property landscaper and maintenance man, as well as being a part-time homemaker. Martha and I agreed that, since I was retired, this was a good time for me to become a *full-time* homemaker. So I said thanks, but no thanks to MBT's generous offer.

I believe it was around 1976, after I retired, that we took up skiing at Mont-Tremblant, in Canada. Brother Glen and his wife Barbara sometimes joined us. Mont-Tremblant is a great ski area with an excellent ski school. Martha and I attended one-week classes there for seven consecutive years. This is where we really learned to ski, especially what we called 'Blue Ice,' which can be dangerous if you don't know how to do it properly.

Living in Romeo, we were only about a 30-minute drive to the Blue Water Bridge in Port Huron. On the other side of the bridge was Sarnia, in Canada, and highway 401. We would take highway 401 through Toronto all the way to Montreal and spend the night there. Then in the morning we drove the 88 miles up the Laurention Mountains to Mont-Tremblant.

The classes would start on Monday morning. The instructors would separate us into three classes, depending on your ability. On Monday there could be as many as 20 in each class. But people would drop out just about every day. I remember one year when Martha and I were the only two left on Friday and had the instructor all to ourselves. In all those years we never once dropped out of a class.

At the top of the mountain was a one-room huge log cabin. Inside was a very large dance floor with the biggest fireplace I have ever seen, smack dab in the middle of the room. The only way one could get to the cabin was by a chair lift. And this is where we spent Friday night, saying goodbye, drinking wine and singing songs by the fireplace. I never will forget singing *Alouette, Gentille Alouette*, a French-Canadian song. Everyone always had a great time.

When the party was over all the sober skiers skied back down the mountain. All the others were taken down in what we called 'The Basket' by the ski patrol. In the many times we went there the only one in our group ever taken down in the 'Basket' was Brother Glen. And he was the guy that the ski instructor mistakenly assigned the job of making sure that no one in our group got drunk that night.

By now Martha had been promoted many times, and at that time her current job description was 'General Manger of Operating Services,' a state-wide position with a budget in excess of one hundred million dollars annually, and a staff of over 5,000 plus people. But that would soon change.

On one very late cold afternoon at Mont-Tremblant in 1981, bushed, we called it a day, then took our skis off and staggered to our room. As soon as we were inside I crashed on a chair and started to take my boots off, just then the wall phone rang. Martha, being close to the phone, answered. I had just taken one boot off and was unbuckling the other when she hung up. She didn't immediately say anything and, curious, I looked up.

How lucky I was, I thought, she was always so stunning in her ski outfits, and with her rosy cheeks and a lock of hair hanging from her ski hat she was absolutely gorgeous.

When she hung up the phone she silently turned, plopped into the nearest chair and vacantly stared out the window, almost as if she had heard bad news. Thinking it *was* bad news, I asked,

"What's up?"

As if she were awe struck, she said,

"I'm an Assistant Vice President." Just like that. From the look on her face I gathered that she never saw this one coming, and the magnitude of this event had just hit home. She was now Michigan Bell's Assistant Vice President for Personnel Administration.

During one of the very rare occasions that Martha discussed her job, she once told me this story:

While she was an assistant VP she was invited to attend a business luncheon at a very exclusive Detroit men's club. When she tried to enter at the front door she was told that the front entrance was for men only and she would have to use the rear entrance. Her response was, if she couldn't come in the front door, she wasn't coming in at all. The doorman asked her to wait a minute and disappeared. When he returned he let her in. She said she was later told by one of the members that she was the first female to enter the front door, up until that day even members' wives had to go in the back.

CHAPTER TEN

*I*N 1982 AT&T AND THE DEPARTMENT OF JUSTICE settled a long-running antitrust case in which AT&T agreed to break itself up in 1984. As a result, seven of what were then known as 'Baby Bells' were created. One of those seven Baby Bells would be the parent company of five telephone companies: Illinois Bell, Michigan Bell, Ohio Bell, Wisconsin Bell and Indiana Bell. The headquarters of this parent company would be located in Chicago.

AT&T would keep Western Electric but would change WECO's name to AT&T Technologies. Later AT&T spun AT&T Technologies off, and their name was changed again, this time to Lucent Technologies. Then, in 2006 Lucent and Alcatel, a French firm, merged and the company is now called Alcatel-Lucent, with its headquarters based in Paris.

In my opinion, the biggest loss to the United States was the loss of Western Electrics Bell Laboratories, which, under AT&T, was the greatest research organization in the world. From its inception Bell Labs had produced seven Nobel prize winners, invented the high-vacuum tube, which ushered in the electronic age, went on to develop the loudspeaker, which brought sound to motion pictures and invented the transistor, the Laser, calculators and **many** other things that changed mankind and boosted America's economy ... but, because of the antitrust suit, it now belongs to a foreign country.

Martha's workday was usually nine or ten hours long. Then she had a 28-mile commute. So we rarely had dinner before seven p.m. Over dinner one evening, in 1982, she told me that Dave Eastlick, then president of Michigan Bell, had asked her that day if she would like to go to Chicago on a temporary transfer for one year to help establish the Human Resources, Compensation and Benefits functions plan for the new Baby Bell.

She would be put up in a furnished condo in the Newberry Plaza building on State Street in Chicago, and Michigan Bell would fly her home and back every weekend. She said that she would miss me dearly, but this was a great opportunity and she felt that she could not turn it down. She would be leaving soon, but would call me every night.

I was used to her being out of town for conferences, but no longer than a week or two at a time. My heart sank when I thought of doing this for a *whole year*. My only consolation was that she would be home on weekends, and there was always the telephone. Of course I would miss her, but having worked for a corporation for so many years I also knew that one just didn't turn down such an opportunity.

As it turned out, by the end of the year the new company was named Ameritech, and William (Bill) Weiss, past president of Illinois Bell, was named Chairman of the Board.

One Friday night, just before Martha's year was up, when I picked her up at the airport, as I usually did, on the way home she told me that Bill Weiss had asked her if she would like to stay on as a full Vice President of Ameritech. I believed that this could very well make her the first female VP of a Fortune 500 company, an historical opportunity for her.

I was completely awe struck and unprepared for this news. It meant that we would have to sell our house in Carriage Hills and move to Chicago. Of course I would miss all my friends here, but this was going to be a life changing event for both of us, and I was extremely proud of her.

So it happened one day, in 1983, after we sold our house, that I said good bye to my many friends and neighbors in the area. Then my 15-pound black French Poodle Gypsy and I left our home in Washington Township (Miss-T had gone to dog heaven a few years before) and drove to Chicago to join my true love.

We soon found a place of our own. It was a condo in a great location in unincorporated Northbrook called 'Mission Hills.' Mission Hills is a beautiful gated community near Northbrook Mall and the train station. Martha would be able to commute by car or train. Condos and townhomes surrounded a beautiful golf course. And now I had more time to work on my memoirs, which I had titled "*Twenty-Seven-Eighty Blues*".

One of the first things I had to do was find a good doctor. I was being treated for high blood pressure in Michigan and had no doctor to write prescriptions for me in Chicago. Ameritech's doctor was Doctor Eneway, brother of the Senator of Hawaii, so Martha asked him for a recommendation. He recommended a Doctor Cape, in nearby Highland Park.

On my first visit to Doctor Cape I was asked to fill out a form regarding my medical history. While reading this form, the Doctor asked;

"Are you still skiing?"

"Yes."

"I see that last summer at 59 you were playing competitive softball?"

"Yes."

"Have you ever had a stress test?"

"No."

"You say here that your father and his father died of heart attacks at 65. With your family history, and skiing at high altitudes in very cold weather, I think we should see how your heart reacts under stress. Shall we do a stress test?"

"You're the doctor."

"Is that a yes?"

"Yes."

The stress test was performed in Doctor Cape's office the following week and the results were not good. Doctor Cape then suggested an angiogram, which I agreed to. An angiogram is a procedure where a dye is injected into an artery while you are awake. The procedure is taped and analyzed later.

Two weeks later Martha and I were in Northwestern Hospital in Chicago where I underwent this procedure. The whole procedure could be seen on a monitor. I was told that I could watch it or not. I decided to watch the dye as it traveled through my arteries, but I could make no sense of the outcome.

I could make sense of it later when the doctor performing the procedure took Martha and me to a room and showed us the results on the monitor, where he could stop it and point out the arteries that were in trouble. There were three, and we could see just how bad they were.

Later that day a conference was held in my hospital room. Besides Martha and me, Doctor Cape was there along with the doctor that performed the angiogram and the doctor that headed up Northwestern Hospital's Cardiology unit. They said that I had two options: angioplasty or bypass surgery. But it was their opinion that I was a good candidate for angioplasty (ballooning to crush the plaque). I then asked, "Who would do it?" The doctor that did my angiogram said that he would.

"How many of these procedures have you done?" I asked.

"Sixty," he said.

"Do I have time to think about it?"

"Yes … but I would recommend that you do it soon," said the head cardiologist.

A few days later I met with Doctor Cape in his office …

"I don't like the fact that this guy has only done sixty of these things," I said. "If it were you what would you do?" I asked.

"Well, there *is* a doctor in Kansas City who has

done thousands, and he does multiple arteries; this doctor only does one. Do you want to go to Kansas City?"

Soon after that Martha and I were in the Heart Hospital in Kansas City. I checked in and successfully underwent the procedure on all three arteries. Because I had this procedure done though, Dr. Cape wanted me to do a stress test every year, which I readily agreed too.

Martha, as always, was wonderful; I never would have made it without her. She made all of the travel arrangements and was by my side giving me moral support through the whole event. I have thought, many times since, what if Martha had not been transferred to Chicago?

CHAPTER ELEVEN

IT WAS NEW YEAR'S EVE, 1983, when Martha and I registered at The Whitehall Hotel just off of One Magnificent Mile in downtown Chicago. I changed into a tuxedo and Martha changed into one of her best outfits. She was absolutely stunning. We then took a cab to the Planetarium, which had been rented by Ameritech just for this occasion. There was not a prouder man there that night than I, when I stepped out of that cab and we went arm in arm into the Planetarium. The officers of all five telephone companies were there as well as those from Ameritech.

This was going to be their big night. At 12:01, 1984, Ameritech would officially become the Holding Company of Illinois Bell, Ohio Bell, Michigan Bell, Indiana Bell and Wisconsin Bell Telephone Companies.

After everyone arrived we were seated in the Planetarium and the show began. The lights dimmed and we tilted our seats back so we could look up at the universe in the huge dome above us. A man's voice droned from above, calling our attention to various stars, and suddenly a lone star streaked out of nowhere above us as the voice from above said …
"AND THEN THERE'S AMERITECH!"

At that same moment the ball in Manhattan stopped falling and we were now in 1984. Nineteen-eighty-three was history and we were now in a new era. At that very moment Ameritech officially became a Fortune 500 company.

Also, I believe, at that same moment, Martha L. Thornton became the first female Vice President of a Fortune 500 company.

***

When I was a young boy, I heard stories of how my 45-year-old great-great grandfather, Sam Thornton, left Okaw, Illinois (now called Arcola) in 1850 and went west in a wagon train over the Santa Fe Trail to look for gold in California. After he made his fortune, so the story goes, he intended to return to his wife, Barbara, better known as 'Barby,' and their ten children he left behind ... but he never came back.

Whenever I think of him, I wonder, 'what happened?' Did he die of natural causes, as one of his partners told it? Or was he murdered by his partners, as Sam's wife Barby believed? Was he killed by Indians, as some in the family say? Or perhaps he met another woman in California and decided to stay there ... another's theory.

Since I was now living in Illinois just a couple of hours away from Arcola, my father's birthplace, I had this irresistible impulse to see the town my father was born and raised in. I mentioned my 'irresistible impulse' to Martha and she said, "Why not?" And that settled it. The impulse soon became a fascinating adventure that took me to the sleepy little town that

Sam, and my father, left behind.

Looking at a map I saw that Arcola was in Union County, not very far south of Champagne-Urbana, home of Illinois University. I figured that if I left soon after Martha went to work, I could be back by the time she got home. Martha, a lover of mysteries herself, said, "Don't worry if you're late coming home, we can always eat out." So the next morning my Nikon camera and I set out on a genealogical adventure I will never forget.

I entered Arcola just in time for lunch. With all the horse and buggies around, my first impression was that this was mostly an Amish town. Each buggy displayed a large red triangle affixed to its rear. The sign reflected light, so a car coming up from behind the buggy at night could not miss seeing it in the dark.

It looked to me like the town wasn't much more than five or six blocks long. Looking around I saw that I had parked near a nice-looking Amish restaurant, so I went in and not only had an excellent lunch, but I also learned from the friendly waitress where the post office was. It was there, I believed, that I would find out if any Thorntons still lived in the area.

After lunch I was told at the post office that a Craig Thornton had an insurance agency two blocks from the post office. Finding his office was easy. He was in, and when I introduced myself and told him I was looking for information about my great-great grandfather, Sam, who went to the goldfields in 1850, he shook my hand and said, "Welcome to

Arcola *cousin!*" Then he opened a drawer in his desk and took out a book. The title was "*The Genealogy of John Thornton*", a book assembled by Roy and Ann Thornton, cousins who lived in St. Louis, Craig said. As I held this book in my hands, I had no idea that it was going to help kick off my newfound writing career.

Ann was a retired librarian, with expertise in genealogy, and Roy and Ann had spent many vacations and thousands of hours researching and putting the John Thornton book together. Craig only had one copy, he said, but he could give me Ann and Roy's address and telephone number if I wanted to see if they had a spare copy.

Then he took me on a quick tour of cemeteries where Thorntons were buried. There were cemeteries in Arcola, nearby Chesterville and Bourbon. The only Thornton buried in the Bourbon cemetery was Sam's wife, Barby. She had been blind for four years before she died at 75 in 1880.

It was getting late and I had to leave. I thanked Craig for taking the afternoon off for the tour and promised him that I would return, and then I headed for Northbrook. On the drive home I was thrilled at what I had seen and heard today, and was anxious to tell Martha all about it. Today's trip only fueled my desire to learn more about my genealogy.

Martha wasn't home yet so I called St. Louis as soon as I got in. Ann Thornton answered the phone. She was delighted to hear from me, and very interested in what I had to say, because, she said, she and Roy had been unable to trace Sam, the youngest of the John Thornton clan after he left Pennsylvania. She said that she would send me a book, and she and Roy would be happy to provide me with any help they could.

When Martha arrived home we decided to eat at 'Two Guys From Italy,' our favorite Italian restaurant nearby. Over dinner I filled Martha in on my exciting day and concluded with, "Some weekend we have *got* to go there." She said she would love to.

We received the "John Thornton" book about a week later. It took me two or three days to just browse through it. It is chock full of copies of original documents ... such as, among other things, a copy of the John Thornton Will, and his actual pay stubs from the Continental Army. He was born in 1758 and served in General Henry Knox's Artillery Brigade at the age of 19. He was also a survivor of Valley Forge. That makes me and my boys Sons of the American Revolution (SAR).

A few months later a group of descendants of John Thornton met in Arcola. Besides Martha and myself, there was Brother Glen and his wife Barbara, Roy and Ann from St. Lewis, my Aunt Florence, my father's sister, who was born and raised in Arcola, and Craig. We spent some time in the cemeteries, and later Aunt Florence took us on a surprise visit to meet her 95-year-old Aunt Sulie (meaning Ursula).

Aunt Sulie was a very interesting woman. She had lived here all her life. When she was a little girl, she said, many Indians lived in the area.

Roy and Anne told us the strange story of how

Arcola got its name. In 1853, they said, the residents and businessmen in the area were dismayed when the Illinois Central Railroad Company decided to go through Okaw and not the town of Fillmore, as they expected. The residents of Okaw then renamed their town at the request of the railroad company. They changed it from Okaw to Arcola, which it is today.

Not to be outdone, the people of Fillmore, the town everyone expected the railroad to go through, changed their name to Bourbon. When the railroad arrived many businesses and homes were physically moved from Bourbon to Arcola, including one two-story building. The Bourbon we visited in 1983 was practically a ghost town at the time. These are just some of the things that make genealogy a nightmare, Roy and Anne said. For example, Barby was a resident of Okaw when Sam left for the gold fields, but a resident of Arcola when she died, yet she never moved.

Another thing was the fact that the names of the townships were often changed. As townships grew they were split. For example, John Thornton's farm was originally in Penn Township, then Mahantango Township, then Chapman Township … and is now in Union Township. According to the U.S. censuses, the same John Thornton lived in all of those townships … but he never moved from his farm.

CHAPTER TWELVE

BACK HOME MARTHA WAS SUPPOSED TO ATTEND A CONFERENCE IN OJAI (Ohigh), California one night and I was alone with Gypsy. I was reading and taking notes from the John Thornton book when the phone rang. I wasn't surprised when I heard Martha on the other end. She took the company plane and must be in Ojai by now, I thought. I was expecting her call but not until later, and I thought she was calling from her room, but I was wrong; she was calling from her rental car with her cell phone.

"I think I'm lost Sweetie," she said. "It's getting dark out, I'm somewhere out in the country and there are no street lights."

"Didn't you get instructions when you rented the car?" I asked.

"Yes, but according to them I should be there by now," she said.

"Give it a few more minutes and I'll stay on the line," I suggested. I had hardly finished when she said, "THERE IT IS! The sign can't be more than two feet off the ground, but I can see lights back in the woods, I'm turning in now, talk to you later Sweetie."

"OK, Honey Bun."

I noticed that Johnny Carson was still on, and then Gypsy jumped off the couch, went to the front door and looked back at me … I knew what that meant, so I got her leash, picked her up and headed for the elevator.

All during our marriage, whenever Martha was out of town on company business, she *never* failed to call me to say goodnight.

Martha was at another conference one night, this time it was in Boca Raton, so I made some pop corn, opened a bottle of Heineken and was reading the John Thornton book again. I decided to write an historical fiction book about it someday. I had barely gotten started when the phone rang. It was my true love. She sounded frightened. She said that she had just gotten in bed when she saw this huge spider in the corner of the ceiling. Martha had a real fear of *any* kind of spider. At home, whenever I heard her scream, "***Robert***," I would grab a newspaper or fly swatter and come running.

That night she said she had called the desk and they promised to send someone up to her room, but that had been fifteen minutes ago and she was afraid the spider would move. I should have known better, but I asked her if she had anything to hit it with. Her response was, "***Are you crazy, I'm not getting out of this bed!***"

Just then I heard a knock on her door, and she said, "Come in." Then I heard her tell someone where the spider was … I heard a *swat*, and she yelled "***He missed it.***" I then heard a *swat, swat*, and a man's voice say, "Its dead, ma'am." Martha, very sweetly, said, "Thank you," and I heard the door close.

"Goodnight Sweetie. I love you," she said.

"I love you too Honey Bun. Goodnight."

Over dinner one night in 1985, Martha mentioned the fact that she had received a letter from Mayor Washington that day thanking her for some work she had done for Chicago regarding Human Resources. She did not elaborate, and it was always my policy not to pursue such statements unless she mentioned them. She kept the letter though, and I still have the original copy.

Two years later, On November 25, 1987, we decided to do some shopping on 'One Mag Mile,' Martha's favorite place to shop in Chicago. We decided to first have lunch at Spiaggia, on Michigan Avenue, another one of our favorite restaurants.

After lunch we walked down Michigan Avenue on our way to our first stop, Bloomingdale's. Just as we approached the store we saw a long caravan of police cars and an ambulance with sirens blasting away, they were slowly coming toward us on the other side of Michigan Avenue. We stopped and watched as the caravan turned and proceeded in the direction of Northwestern Hospital.

When they disappeared, we entered Bloomingdale's. As we headed toward the escalators we saw a group of employees watching a television set. Martha asked them what was going on, they said that Mayor Washington had just had a heart attack, and they were taking him to the hospital. We did not learn that the attack was fatal until we heard the five o'clock news at home. Martha made no comment about it at the time, and again, I did not pursue it.

One of our favorite seafood restaurants in Chicago in those days was Shaw's Crab House at 21 E. Hubbard.

One day we had a dinner date with Frank and Faye Zimmerman at Shaw's. We were walking and had to go through the underpass at Michigan Avenue. The famous Billy Goat Tavern was down there and we had to walk right past it. We weren't far from Shaw's and we were early, so we decided to have a glass of wine in the Tavern just so we could say that we had been there.

At the bar the bartender asked us what he could do for us, and Martha said she would like a Chardonnay. The bartender's response was …

"Lady, we have two kinds of wine, 'white' and 'red.'" So she said, "White." Then he put a water glass in front of her, produced a large jug of white wine, filled her glass, and as it was glug, glug, glugging, he asked me what I wanted. I said …

"Red," and he repeated the procedure. But now we could at last say we had been to the Billy Goat Tavern!

CHAPTER THIRTEEN

WHILE LIVING IN MISSION HILLS we decided to expand our skiing horizons by going west where the powder was. Snow out west is light and powdery whereas, in the Midwest and East Coast, it is heavier and sometimes icy. As far as I know there is no ice in the western states.

We tried Colorado, and loved Vail, but the two-and-one-half-hour drive through the mountains, sometimes in snow storms, could sometimes be hair-raising. When we tried Park City, Utah, we thought it was more convenient for us. We could fly from Chicago directly to Salt Lake City, rent a car, and 45 minutes later we were in Park City. It was just what we were looking for. So we bought a condo on Deer Valley Road, about five or ten minutes from the Deer Valley slopes to our left, and about the same to the Park City slopes to our right.

Stein Ericson, skiing's first superstar, is the director of skiing at the Deer Valley Resort and he is also the host of the magnificent Stein Ericson Lodge as of this writing. We first heard of Stein many years ago when he was a ski instructor in Michigan.

The Stein Ericson Lodge is located at mid-mountain in Deer Valley, and is home of the four-star restaurant, the Glitretind. You can ski in and ski out of the lodge, which makes it easy to have lunch there, relax, and people-watch. It is almost like a fashion show. Most diners were wearing the latest in ski wear. Many movie stars and celebrities have homes nearby.

Park City is built on a fairly steep side of a mountain. Main Street is bordered by great restaurants and shops. It slopes down the side of the mountain, ending a few blocks from our condo. When it came to skiing though, we preferred Deer Valley, with its impeccably groomed slopes and amenities. However, we spent most of our free time in the great restaurants and shops in Park City. Park City is also host to Robert Redford's Sundance Film Festival every winter.

In the summer a band shell is set up at the foot of the Deer Valley slopes and people come from everywhere with wine and fried chicken to sit on the grass and watch the Utah Symphony Orchestra perform every weekend. Our condo was so close to Deer Valley we would grab a blanket and walk to the performances in minutes.

***

On July 5, 1989, an announcement in the Wall Street Journal *and the* New York Times *said that Ameritech had named Martha Thornton as their 'Corporate* **Senior** *Vice President, Human Resources.' This would be her last and biggest breaking of a glass ceiling. She would serve Ameritech in this capacity until she retired in 1994.*

***

I rarely knew of most of her promotions until long after they happened. And when I did, it was usually from other people. She rarely talked about them, or herself. One could know her for years and never find out about her many accomplishments from her. If someone asked her if she worked, she would simply answer that she worked for the telephone companies and that would be the end of it. I'm sure she never thought about breaking glass ceilings. I don't think she wanted to prove anything. I do believe her aim was to always do what she thought was in the best interest of her employer. She was a lifetime member of the NAACP and was never a 'woman's libber.'

I knew she did not believe in 'tooting her own horn.' Yet, she never seemed to mind, and never once objected, if *I* talked about her accomplishments. When I did, I believe she knew it was because I was so proud of her, and I believe that she understood. The glint in her eyes and smile on her face when I did praise her in the presence of others told me that it was OK for me to do what she could not. In the thirty-nine and a half years that we were married and the three years we went together before that, I *never once* had any doubt that she loved me. She showed me in so many ways.

I think one of her best attributes was her ability to separate her job from the rest of her life. I think that when she was at work she was incredibly good. But she rarely brought her work home. When she was home, all she wanted to do was to be a good mother, wife and human being, and she was extremely good at those. I think that one of her many assets was that she was *unflappable*. She was *always* very calm and cool headed. *Nothing* seemed to visibly upset her. In all of our married life I *never* saw her lose her temper. Another asset that we both possessed was *'Trust'* with a capitol 'T.' With Martha being gone on so many extended business trips our marriage would never have survived very long without our trusting each other.

Besides Dianne, me and her job, the things Martha loved most were her home, skiing, music, bridge and the theater, just to mention a few ... *She just loved life.*

I was once asked ... what did she say about the articles in the *Wall Street Journal* and *New York Times*? My answer is simple ... nothing! Even I never knew about most of them until I found them while doing research for this book. She just never thought of it as a big deal.

***

In 1989 we moved to 54 Oak Creek Court in Burr Ridge, Illinois. The developer of Mission Hills had sold his last units and wanted to get out of the development. All he had to do now was sell the golf course. He had given the homeowners the first right of refusal. The only problem was, according to the Homeowners By-Laws, it took 65 percent of the homeowners to approve the sale, and when they voted on the subject they only got 64 percent of the votes.

So the developer sold the course to a corporation, who then turned it into a public course. We felt that our security was compromised and property values would soon tumble, so we sold our condo and moved to a townhome in Burr Ridge.

After living in a condo for over five years we found that we just didn't like condo living. For one thing, we had to haul groceries and other supplies up four stories, sometimes in a crowded elevator, then down a very long hallway to our unit.

Then there was Gypsy. Every time she had to

go out we had to carry her to the elevator, hope it wasn't crowded, take her outside—no matter what the weather—and then, after she took her sweet time getting around to her business, we had to make the same trip back again to our unit upstairs. And another: we had two cars and only one parking space indoors. Guess who had to clean the snow and ice off of a freezing cold car in the winter ... not that it wasn't the right thing to do. Everything considered, we felt like we were living in a hotel, only worse.

In Burr Ridge, we lived in a three-story townhome with twice the square feet and a three-car attached garage. Also, I could really do some serious writing there since nearby Hinsdale had a great library that I could do research in.

We were in a gated community called the Oak Creek Club, 17.5 miles from Chicago on 91st Street, between County Line Road and 83rd St. Martha could commute or drive. When I was required to attend social functions downtown with Martha I could take the train and meet her at the Mercantile Exchange building, then drive home with her afterword.

We were just a few miles from Oakbrook Mall and I loved the great restaurants there. So I spent many afternoons having lunch and shopping in the Mall. Martha and I did the same on many a Saturday or Sunday. Sometimes on weekends we even took in a movie there.

While living in Burr Ridge we joined an athletic club. I used the club almost every day. It was hard for Martha to use it except on weekends. Martha was an early bird; she always left for work at 4:30 a.m. So on weekends she wanted to work out early.

The club opened at 5:30 a.m. So we had to be at the club when they opened the doors. We were always the first car in the parking lot, usually five or ten minutes before the doors opened. The weather could be freezing cold, or it could be snowing or raining, but it didn't matter—we were there waiting.

When the person with the keys showed up, we would get out of the car and be waiting at the door as it was unlocked. On weekends we were always the first members there. God love her, I never once complained. I was so proud to be able to say that she was my wife.

CHAPTER FOURTEEN

*O*N SEPTEMBER 16, 1990, MARTHA'S *PICTURE WAS IN THE* CHICAGO TRIBUNE *along with an announcement that she had been elected to the board of directors of the Old Kent Financial Corp., a multibank holding company based in Grand Rapids, Michigan. I believed that this was quit a feather in her cap.*

In early 1991 President Bill Clinton was trying to get a United Healthcare bill passed through Congress. At the same time Senator Ted Kennedy, heading up a U.S. Senate Committee on Labor and Human Resources, was holding hearings on the subject. As Senior Vice President of Human Resources for Ameritech, Martha was, at that time, considered one of the top people in that field.

As usual, we rarely discussed our work at home, but this was one of those rare occasions, like when she was going to be interviewed on CNN and she asked me to tape it (I still have that tape). One night in early January Martha said,

"Next week I'm going to Washington; I've been asked to testify before a hearing of Ted Kennedy's Select Committee on Healthcare next week (January 10, 1991). I should be back on Friday. I'm taking the company plane."

We never discussed her testimony when she came home, but she did have something to say about one

of the Senators. Some of her comments are better left
unsaid. She did get thank-you letters for testifying
from Senator Kennedy and Illinois Senator Paul
Simon.

Through hours of research I found the following
information on the Internet, and now ... I know the
rest of the story. The complete story can be found
in the Cornell University Library. On the Internet it
can be found under "The Health Care Crisis and the
American Family."

The committee was chaired by Senator **Edward
Kennedy** from Massachusetts. Senators on the
committee included:

Orrin Hatch, Utah
Howard Metzenbaum, Ohio
Nancy Kassebaum, Kansas
Christopher Dodd, Connecticut
James Jeffords, Vermont
Paul Simon, Illinois
Tom Harkin, Iowa
Strom Thurmond, South Carolina
Brock Adams, Washington
Dave Durenberger, Minnesota
Barbara Mikulski, Maryland
Thad Cochran, Mississippi
Jeff Bingaman, New Mexico and
Paul Wellstone, Minnesota

I believe the following to be the actual minutes,
which may include some grammatical, and or typing
errors. These are only the minutes that concern

Martha's testimony.

Senator **Edward Kennedy**, chairman of the Senate Committee on Labor and Human Resources is speaking:

Senator Kennedy;

"Our next panel is a distinguished group of experts which represents a range of perspectives on the need for major health care reform. We welcome **Martha Thornton**, who is senior vice president of human resources for Ameritech Corporation; Senior Vice President, Ameritech, Chicago, Il; Gail Shearer, Manager Policy Analysis, Consumers Union, Washington, DC; Dr. Alan R. Nelson, Immediate Past President American Medical Association, Salt Lake City, UT; and Lena Archuleta, Member, Board of Directors, American Association of Retired Persons, Denver CO. We'll start with **Ms. Thornton.**"

Martha then provided an oral statement followed be a prepared statement which she then turned over to the committee. I have omitted the oral statement due to its length and the fact that most of the points she made in the oral statement are also covered in the prepared statement.

Prepared Statement by **Martha L. Thornton**

The Federal Government should encourage the development and use of organized delivery systems as the preferred way to offer quality medical Care and to control rising health care costs. New private sector approaches, such as organized delivery systems bring employers, employees, and health care providers together in a cooperative effort.

Organized delivery systems consist of physicians, hospitals, and others linked by a commitment to deliver quality medical services to a particular group, such as a company's employees. This system unites the employer, the managed care intermediary, and the health care providers to find common solutions to the problems of cost, quality, and access to care.

Ameritech, a large communications company, headquartered in the Midwest, has adopted a managed health care plan, one type of organized delivery system. Our plan encourages employees to choose from physicians and hospitals in a network offered by the company's health plan administrator. Preferred providers agree up front to negotiated fees and certain medical management programs. Employees using these preferred providers are able to minimize their out-of-pocket medical expenses.

Ameritech's managed care plan has
allowed the company to improve patient
care and to realize below average growth
in health care costs without shifting
costs to employees. One of the seven
regional communications companies
formed as a result of the breakup of the
Bell System. In 1989, our net income was
$1.2 billion. The company has 76,000
active employees, predominantly in five
states: Illinois, Indiana, Michigan,
Ohio, and Wisconsin. In addition,
we have 45,000 retired employees.
Ameritech provides medical coverage to
all active and retired employees, and
their dependents, approximately 250,000
people in total.

Our employee population has some
interesting characteristics. It is an
older work force, with an average age
of 41.4 years. The average employee has
17 years experience with the company.
Retirees leave the company with 32
years of service, on average, and at an
average age of 57 years.

These service characteristics combined
with our commitment to provide medical
benefits, makes management of medical
benefits a priority for us.

In 1989, the company spent $337 million
on health care, of which almost $100
million was for retirees and their
dependents. Total expenses were 13.3

percent more than in 1988. For the
5-year period ending in 1989, our annual
increase averaged 10.4 percent, which
represents less of an increase than
for many other employers and general
insurance industry trends.

We have accomplished this by focusing on
the effectiveness of our expenditures
and not shifting costs to our employees.
We have had the cooperation of our
employees and the two unions which
represent many of our employees, the
Communications Workers of America
and the International Brotherhood of
Electrical Workers.

Ameritech has been actively involved
in health care policy issues for
several years. At the federal level,
we are represented on the Board of the
Washington Business Group on Health. As
part of that group, we testified before
Rep. Waxman's health subcommittee
about proposed changes to the federal
Health Maintenance Organization (HMO)
Act. We are also active in the National
Association of Manufacture's, the U.S.
Chamber of Commerce, and the National
Leadership Coalition for Health Care
Reform.

THE PROBLEM OF ACCESS

The annual increases faced by some
companies have forced them to curtail

health care coverage. State governments have tightened both eligibility requirements and reimbursement levels for public programs. These actions reduce access for the poor. Changes in Medicare reimbursement policy have placed a greater financial burden on the private sector through cost shifting. This is a hidden tax burden on the sick and those paying for care, which is not spread equitably across all taxpayers. As coverage becomes more difficult to obtain, care does as well.

Providing residents of this country with adequate health care protection is a policy goal which Ameritech fully supports. Achieving this goal is a complex matter involving a number of distinct but interrelated issues such as the extent of coverage available, the quality of care, and financing of care for the poor, to name a few. Although it is necessary to focus separately on each issue when developing legislative initiatives, it is equally important to place the interrelationships into the broad context of competing national goals.

Ameritech believes that employment-based approaches are the preferred vehicle to expand coverage. While employers can help employees, the ultimate responsibility must rest with the individual. We know from other employers that even in the presence of a plan provided and primarily funded by the employer, some employees choose to forego coverage. Employers should not be penalized for choices made independently by employees.

We must find ways to make coverage affordable for smaller employers and individual purchasers of health care plans. In particular, small groups must be able to benefit from the managed care programs available to larger groups. In addition, the many state laws which mandate coverage for particular classes of providers or treatments must be reviewed. Many of these mandates add to the cost of coverage without adding commensurately to the benefits to be gained.

To expand access to private plans for individuals not presently covered, we should be prepared to subsidize low-income groups to help ease the burden for them to purchase health coverage. In addition, individuals and unincorporated businesses must receive the same tax exclusion for medical benefits as for incorporated businesses.

Health care cost control has been an elusive goal for government, employers, labor, and individual consumers. We are all part of the problem, therefore we must be part of the solution.

Increasing access is very important, but cannot be discussed without attention to cost and quality of care issues.

ORGANIZED DELIVERY SYSTEMS — CONTROLLING COST AND IMPROVING ACCESS AND QUALITY

The existing medical delivery system is highly fragmented among various types of providers and sites of care. This inhibits coordination of services to patients, as there is no central person or organization taking full responsibility for managing all that occurs during a particular case." Most importantly, quality management and quality improvement activities cannot be carried out effectively under the current fragmented system. This is particularly true of care occurring in physician offices.

The Federal Government should encourage the development and use of organized delivery systems as the preferred way to deliver medical care and medical benefits. Such systems would be expected to supplant the current, fragmented regime.

Organized delivery systems consist of physicians, hospitals, and others tied together by a commitment to deliver services effectively and efficiently to a given population, such as employees of a company, or beneficiaries of a government program.

The organization and its providers commit to continuous quality improvement aimed not just at the delivery of services, but, more importantly, aimed at improving the health status of the population being served.

Ameritech and many other national employers are heading in this direction, as are the national insurers, Blue Cross plans, and others. It is also the direction that public programs should be moving.

For Ameritech, it means building on those aspects of our current plan which have contributed to lower than average growth in costs. This includes using the medical management and negotiated provider reimbursements of our local Blue Cross plans.

Under the current plan, Blue Cross reviews medical care received by our employees and their dependents. All elective hospital admissions are reviewed prospectively for appropriateness of the procedure and for the site of service. All admissions, whether urgent or elective, are reviewed for appropriateness of continued stay while the patient is hospitalized.

While control of hospital usage is

important for cost control, quality is also of concern. Patients receive valuable assistance selecting personally appropriate treatments and procedures.

Organized delivery systems improve patient care as well as help control expenses. For example, recently, physicians recommended hysterectomies for several Young women who are beneficiaries of our plan. These women were referred to other physicians by Blue Cross nurses and underwent non-surgical alternative treatments. These treatments alleviated their problems, and allowed them to become pregnant and first-time mothers. Had they followed the original surgical recommendation, pregnancy would not have been possible.

Our plan also provides to employees the option of using a preferred provider network, which gives employees financial incentives to use selected physicians and hospitals. These providers have agreed to accept negotiated fee schedules, and to voluntarily adhere to medical management programs of Blue Cross. This program has helped control the growth in provider reimbursements of our plans.

The plan covers pre-natal care, well child care, and a select group of early detection services for adults. These should have a positive payback, although over the long term.

We cannot rest on past success. We recently announced that employees will be offered a new plan — called an open ended HMO or Point of Service plan. This type of plan is becoming increasingly popular among large employers. National insurers, Blue Cross plans, or large health maintenance organizations, put together networks of providers, and the systems necessary to manage cost, utilization, and quality of services rendered to eligible individuals. While individuals have the option of using the physician or hospital of their choice, there will be incentives to use those participating in the network.

The physicians, hospitals, and ancillary providers are chosen according to criteria which examine their qualifications, such as Board certification, and their agreement to participate in medical management and quality improvement activities. The physicians, in particular, must be willing to have their office practices scrutinized by the networks.

This approach is the first step towards the widespread adoption of the organized delivery systems referenced earlier. It binds together the employer, the managed care intermediary and the providers, to find common solutions to the problem of cost, quality and access to care. There will be less need for employers, or others acting on their behalf, to police the practice of medicine of participating physicians, or the delivery of services in hospitals. The providers will be performing this role as part of their contract, and their belief in the need for peer oversight.

Organized delivery systems and managed care should be made available to smaller employers and be adopted for government programs as well.

Ameritech's senior management believes that these systems will enable us to better control our cost growth into the future without shifting costs to our employees. At the same time, our employees will have access to quality medical care and a quality benefit package.

A NEW MODEL OF CONSUMER CHOICE

The rise of organized delivery systems will allow employers to offer benefits programs which can be cost effective, yet promise better quality of care than the current fee-for-service system.

Employees will be able to choose from systems preselected by their employer.

Employers will use competition among

competing delivery systems to maximize
the value of our expenditures and those
of our employees. The competition
to satisfy the employer and the
employee will stimulate innovation and
improvement of the delivery of care and
the delivery of medical benefits.

Choice will not be the freedom to select
from any and all plans or providers in
a community, but from a smaller group
pre-selected by one's employer, trust
fund, or government program. This new
concept of choice will be the only way
to assure a balance of cost control,
access, and quality of care.

THE ROLE OF GOVERNMENT

Government's primary role should be
the creation of a legislative and
regulatory structure which encourages
certain activities and inhibits others,
consistent with desired social policy.
The Federal Government must set the
parameters and ground rules within which
we operate. Other principles of the
government's role should include the
following: laws encouraging utilization
review, selective contracting
arrangements, and other managed care
approaches will help the development of
organized delivery system. Government
should not micro-manage the health care
delivery system or the benefits delivery
system, except to protect the health

and safety of the public.

Government must continue to be the safety net for those without the financial means to access such plans. In addition, it should remain the primary payer for the elderly through the Medicare program. As stated earlier, we support the use of private health plans as the vehicle to expand coverage, and therefore access.

Government programs should be financed appropriately. Financing should be explicit and widely based. Use of taxes or surcharges on those with medical plans, such as premium taxes, or taxes on medical services, should be eliminated. This includes use of "All Payer" systems which place surcharges on hospital or physician bills to pay for uncompensated care.

Government must purchase health care, such as is done by the private sector. It should not shift its financial responsibilities to the private sector, nor should it use its legislative powers to systematically underpay providers.

Information is critical to appropriate decision-making, whether one is looking at an individual patient, or at a given population. We need to build on the efforts being made in various states to collect, analyze, and disseminate information about the Price, utilization,

and quality of care. These data should
be from public and private purchasers.

The Federal Government should increase
its support of the evaluation of new
and existing medical technologies.
Technology should be defined in
its broadest sense: equipment,
pharmaceuticals, and procedures or
techniques.

Technology evaluation includes
development of practice guidelines or
practice parameters. This can assist
physicians and other providers of
services to determine what works, or
doesn't work, for particular diseases
in particular patient groups. Put into
language understandable by the patient,
better individual decision-making could
result.

Government support for technology
evaluation studies can help determine
which technologies would be disseminated
to the community, as well as which
would be withdrawn. In addition, payers
can apply the information when making
reimbursement decisions.

The government can help develop
treatment guidelines for needed reform
of the medical malpractice system. It
has been shown in certain areas of
the country that guidelines reduce
malpractice premiums and the practice

of defensive medicine.

Federal initiatives should fund research as well as be a Clearinghouse of results from the private sector. This would include initiatives such as those undertaken by the American Medical Association and various medical specialty societies.

It could also include projects like the planned trial of the Outcomes Management tools championed by Dr. Paul Ellwood. The trial is being conducted by a consortium of large national managed care firms and national employers, including Ameritech. This tool evaluates the effects of medical interventions by measuring the changes in a patient's ability to carry out his or her normal daily activities. From this, we will be able to determine whether the intervention improved, maintained, or decreased the patient's quality of life.

Federal policy should not attempt to find a single approach to apply to all areas of the country, all population, groups, or all medical marketplaces. As we find within our own company, there are differences, and we must provide choices to people.

CONCLUSION

Increasing access to medical care through increased access to medical coverage is a goal fully supported by Ameritech. We believe that the business community wants to cooperate in the development of solutions which can improve the current situation. At least in the short term, we expect this will require increased public and private expenditures.

Access must not be dealt with in a vacuum. Additional reimbursement dollars without any cost controls will exacerbate the current cost spiral. Increased access cannot be accomplished independent of changes to the delivery of care, and without regard to the cost and quality of that care.

Cost control and quality improvement must be part of the solution.

Cost control is important for us and for all American industry as we compete here and abroad for business. While health care is an expense, it can also be viewed as an investment in our human resources. A productive work force is important, and effective health care contributes to building this competitive asset.

New approaches, such as organized delivery systems, bring the interested parties together in a cooperative effort. They do not put employers, government, or other third parties in the role of police officers trying to locate and root out bad apples. Organized delivery systems are showing that controlling costs is compatible with improving quality of care.

Public policy must encourage the development and use of organized delivery systems, which should be the preferred means to improve access for the currently uninsured. Large employers are using this approach for their employees, including senior management. We are not advocating something for others that we are not willing to do ourselves.

The success of organized delivery systems, and cost control in general, will depend on a body of knowledge about the effectiveness of various medical interventions, or the lack thereof. Increased government support of research in this area, and dissemination of results, will be critical.

Government must not use its legislative powers to shift its financial responsibilities onto others. Continued government underfunding of programs, inadequate provider reimbursement, and attempts to micro-manage health care delivery will undermine the private sector's efforts to provide quality health care to employees. We urge use of the same health care purchasing techniques for government beneficiaries as are used in the private sector.

In closing, I would like to thank you again for the opportunity to testify, and to offer our assistance to the members of the committee, and your staff, in better understanding our approach to health care management as well as general trends in the business community. In addition, we would be pleased to work with you through the business organizations in which we have been participating.

CHAPTER FIFTEEN

O N SEPTEMBER 26, 1991, MARTHA WAS
QUOTED IN AN ARTICLE in the *Wall Street Journal* concerning Ameritech's Retirement Plan for its Managers ... By John J. Keller.

Cutting its management work force will enable Ameritech "[to] more effectively respond to our rapidly changing industry and world-wide competition," said Martha L. Thornton, senior vice president for human resources. "Today's increasingly competitive business climate is requiring us to make major shifts in the way we run our business."

At Ameritech, managers who elect to voluntary retire will get an extra three years of age and service credit added to their pension benefits, the company said. And they can receive their pension payments either as lump-sum or monthly payments. To qualify, the managers must leave the payroll by Dec. 31.

In addition, managers must have at least five years of service and be employees of the Ameritech Bell companies. These include Ameritech's five phone companies and units such as Ameritech Information Systems, Ameritech Services, Ameritech Audiotex Services, Ameritech International and Ameritech Mobile Communications. All told, 14 Ameritech units are offering the retirement plan to their managers.

In October of 1991 Martha and I made our first of

many golf trips to Hawaii. While there we took a fascinating helicopter flight over the Big Island.

On February 10, 1992, Martha was quoted in an article in the *New York Times* written by Milt Freudenheim regarding President Bush's Health Plan:

Martha Thornton, a senior vice president in Chicago with Ameritech Corporation, which has 77,000 employees in the Bell telephone companies in the five Midwestern states, said,
   "The most positive thing about the President's proposal is that it offers another alternative in the debate over what should be done."
   She also opposed putting new restrictions on Medicare and Medicaid. But she said the President's plan would indeed help the control the growth of health-care costs by making it easier for small groups to get insurance, limiting payments in medical malpractice lawsuits, and encouraging health maintenance organizations and hospital and physician networks.
   "There's enough money in the system today to finance needed health care, if we control the system," she said.

Then one evening in 1993, when I was putting the finishing touches on dinner, I heard the garage door open and close so I knew that Martha was home. As I was preparing the dinner salad she walked into the kitchen, and as she put her purse down she very casually said that she was retiring. I was taken totally by surprise; she was as cool as a cucumber. Over dinner she said that the Chairman was going to retire soon and she thought it was a good time for her to go too. I was all for it. I was relieved and happy for her. I was happy that she was taking it so well. I was happy because I would soon have a full-time wife and would no longer need an appointment to see her during working hours. What a great day this was for both of us.

Now we had to decide where to spend our retirement years. After carefully considering our options it came down to Florida. Martha's father, brother, sister and stepmother lived in Bradenton and Dianne lived in nearby Ellenton. At that time Dianne was working as a CPA for Tropicana.

We had been going to Florida on vacations for 30 years by then. We never stayed with family members; we stayed out on the islands … Anna Maria, Siesta Key and Longboat Key.

We knew the area very well, and really liked it, so we decided to locate somewhere near Sarasota. The islands were out, we had walked enough beaches. Since we both loved golfing, we decided to locate near, or on, a golf course. After weeks of looking we decided on The Oaks Club in Osprey, between Venice and Sarasota.

The Oaks Club consists of three gated communities now called 'Bayside, 'Clubside' and 'The Preserve.' In 1994, after Martha retired, we built and moved into a house in 'The Preserve' at 143 Bishopscourt, and became 'snow birds' for the next five years, spending summers in Burr Ridge and winters in Florida. When we first started snow-birding, we would leave Florida and fly to Chicago sometime in May, and return to Florida sometime in October.

When we were first married, back in 1967, I became the banker. I was the major breadwinner at the time and I wrote the checks and paid the bills. Back then, that's the way most American families operated. We only had one checking account with both names on the account and *everything* was in both of our names … our house, our cars … everything. In almost 40 years of marriage we never had a problem with that.

When Martha retired and our finances became more complicated I was relieved when she offered to take over the job. And what a good job she did. Besides working with two financial advisers, she loved to buy and sell stocks and bonds on her own, and she was absolutely brilliant at it.
     One good reason we had such a smooth marriage was the fact that we worked so well together. It really was easy; we just seemed to like the same things … add to that the fact that we respected and loved each other, and you have as close to a perfect marriage as you can get.

***

In 1996, I was scheduled to take my annual stress test at Dr. Cape's office in Highland Park, Illinois on September 30th. We had tickets to fly back to Florida on October 3rd. I had passed the test with flying colors now for 12 years and had no reason to believe I would not pass it this year. One can imagine how shocked I was when I didn't. And even more so when Dr. Cape said that I needed bypass surgery and had to go to Northwestern Hospital in Evanston as soon as possible. Stunned, I said …

"OK, let me call Martha and she'll come and take me over there."

"No, you're going in an ambulance, and we'll call Martha," Doctor Cape said.

CHAPTER SIXTEEN

ON OCTOBER 3RD, INSTEAD OF FLYING TO FLORIDA, Martha followed me down the hall to the operating room, kissed me and said "I love you." I said, "I love you too", and I was wheeled into the operating room.

I remember being in a half dream world. It was a horrible dream and when I slowly came out of it Martha was there holding my hand, and the horrible dream slowly, very slowly, faded away.

Then I remember a female nurse coming in. Martha was reading a book. The nurse said that she had to make the bed; she pointed to an empty chair and said that I could sit there while she made the bed.

"I'm sorry," I said, but I can't get out of bed."

"Oh yes you can!" she said. "If you don't, I'll come over there and get you out, but you're not going to like that! Take your choice."

I looked over at Martha for support but she had her eyes glued on her book. I decided that I was getting no help from her, so I very painfully got out of bed.

After I got back in bed the doctors came in and said the usual doctor stuff about how well everything went, etc., etc. Much later Martha said I had to get up and walk around the room. She helped me, and when we went by the window I could look down and see the Northwestern football field. Then I saw a TV up near the corner of the ceiling. Great, I thought. I knew that Michigan was playing Northwestern *here* this Saturday.

Saturday morning, when the nurse made me get out of bed, Martha took me for a walk in the hallway and then around the room again. When we went by the window I looked down and saw the stadium filling with fans. Once back in bed I turned the TV on and watched the game while Martha read her book.

Northwestern had the ball on Michigan's 20-yard line. There were only six seconds to go and Michigan was leading seven to six. Northwestern kicked a field goal and won the game. The whole hospital erupted with cheers; nurses and nurses aids were dancing in the hallways.

I can't recall how long I was in the hospital before I was allowed to go home to Burr Ridge. But once back home I remember Martha dragging me around the cul-de-sac several times each day, then making me blow into some device to make a ping pong ball bounce up and down.

Finally the doctor gave me the OK to fly back to Florida on September 20th. As usual, Martha was a sweetheart through all of this. And I'm afraid I was a baby. She had the patience of an angel, was at the hospital every day and waited on me hand and foot at home. Although she always said that she hated to cook, she actually cooked my meals without complaining, and she really wasn't bad at it. She also did a great job making all the arrangements, and got me back to Florida and Bishopscourt safely all by herself.

After five years of snow-birding we finally decided

to give it up in 1998. About that time Toll Brothers, a builder with a reputation of building quality homes, purchased over 90 lots from the developer on 'Clubside.' We liked one of their models, so we put a deposit on a lot and sold the Burr Ridge Townhome. We then put the house in the 'Preserve' up for sale when Toll Brothers started to build our 'dream house' on MacEwen Drive. We moved in on April 1, 1999, and we loved it. I never saw Martha happier, and when she was happy, I was happy.

When we first moved to The Oaks, Martha joined the Women's Golf Association right away. In my case, I didn't think I was good enough to join the men's league, so I golfed by myself and with Martha on Sundays for the first three years.

As a result, most of our new friends and our social life developed around people Martha met golfing. In those days I was known as Martha's husband. It then occurred to me that I needed to start playing in the men's league if I wanted to find friends of my own. I did, and quickly found out that I was hardly the worst golfer out there.

In the meantime, Martha became president of the Oaks Women's Golf Association for three years, and the Women's Club for two years, and then she was elected to the first Oaks Club Board of Governors after the developer left.

This was no surprise to me. Some of her close friends knew her bio, and there were two members here that were past CEOs of 'Baby Bells' along with several retired officers of telephone companies who knew her by reputation.

Part Two

In Part One of *From "Blues" to Bliss* I describe Martha as the incredibly successful business woman as well as the devoted homemaker that she was. In Part Two, she will be revealed as an incredibly courageous woman while she fought a dreadful terminal disease.

If there is one thing I learned as a combatant in World War II, it is that one can be courageous, but there is no such thing as fearless. I think that the trick is that *everybody feels fear*, but others may never see it, and one must carry on.

Just about everyone has heard the adage that *there are no atheists in fox holes*. In my case, my fox hole was the B17. In the many barracks discussions I participated in concerning the subject, I never met a man who did not confess that, during the heat of combat, he was scared stiff, and no matter what his religious beliefs were, he prayed. But, at the same time, he was able to put that fear aside and do his job.

That is why, I believe, service men are drilled, over and over and over again, until they can do their job automatically. At the time, we thought that was as boring as 'aw-get-out,' but, at that time, we had never experienced actual combat.

If you have ever met a person who says they have no fear of dying, I believe that, at least 99 (plus) percent of them are lying or in denial.

I say this now, because Part Two of *From "Blues" to Bliss* will show her as a perfect example of *real* courage. It was not that Martha had no fear; it was that she was so good at *never* letting *anyone* but me see it. And that even goes for her oncologist. I know, because in those seven years we were practically inseparable.

One of the best examples of what courage and fear can do to a person can be seen in the movie *Twelve O'clock High*, starring Gregory Peck. If you have not seen it yet ... do. I believe that every American should see this movie ... it is a classic. I know this because I was there.

*Note: new procedures for cures and early detection for cancer are always on the horizon, to protect yourself, consult your healthcare provider on a regular basis.

CHAPTER SEVENTEEN

IT ALL STARTED ONE DAY IN THE LATTER PART OF MAY, 1999, when Martha told me that she saw some blood in her urine. The mere fact that she told me worried me. Knowing Martha as I did, I knew that this must have been happening for some time before she told me about it. That's just the way she was … an eternal optimist.

I don't mean to imply that Martha was cavalier about her health. She just had a high tolerance for physical discomfort. I can think of only one day in her entire 30-year career that she took the day off because she was sick. Nevertheless, while she was working, she'd had a complete physical every year. Not that she felt that it was necessary … but because it was a company requirement.

I, on the other hand, was just the opposite. I'm sorry to say that too many times I told Martha about some complaint I had and her standard answer was, "That's nothing, you're OK. Don't worry about it Sweetie." And she was usually right.

Martha had every reason to believe that she was in great shape. Her cholesterol was the envy of everyone. Her HDL was in the *seventies*. Her father died in his mid-eighties, her older brother Al is presently (at the time of writing) eighty-three, Art is eighty-one and her kid sister Helen is sixty-nine.

She always passed her physicals with flying colors.

She worked out regularly and took good care of her health.

Since she had no Urologist, and I thought I had a great one in Doctor Demmler, I made an appointment for her with Dr. Demmler. When she came out of the his office she said that he took a blood test and said he thought it was probably a kidney stone. That sounded logical, so we thought there was no need to worry.

At The Oaks, the Women's Golf Association plays on Tuesdays and Thursdays. The Men's League plays on Wednesdays and Saturdays. Martha played in the Women's Golf Association and also played on Saturday with some friends and Sundays and holidays and couples events with me.

I think it was on a Tuesday when the phone rang while Martha was golfing. It was Doctor Demmler's nurse. She said that the doctor wanted to speak to Martha. I told her that she was playing golf and I would have her call as soon as she came home. The nurse then said …

"No, the Doctor wants to talk to her *now*." I explained to her that the best I could do was to get a Ranger to take me out on the golf course and bring her in.

"Bring her right to the office then," the nurse said.

I called the club house and had them call the Ranger in so he would be there when I arrived. He was waiting for me at the clubhouse and took me right to her foursome, and then I nervously drove a very frightened wife to the doctor's office. I sat in the

waiting room while she entered the office. Moments
later the nurse came out and said that the doctor
wanted to see me. I knew then that this was not a
good omen. And when I entered his office I knew
that our lives would never be the same again.

Martha was sitting in a chair; when she saw me
she immediately stood up. She started crying as we
locked in a fierce embrace. With her head buried in
my shoulder she said that she had cancer and it was
hopeless. I must point out here that this was the only
time *anyone*, with me being the only exception, *ever*
saw her fearful.

"There's always hope Sweetie," I said as I stroked
her hair. "Never give up."

Doctor Demmler said that, just on a hunch, when
Martha first saw him he took a blood test. The test
indicated that she probably had some kind of cancer,
he had no idea what kind, but he wanted to do a CAT
scan at Doctors Hospital ASAP. He said he thought
it best if we did it today. We agreed, and a few hours
later we were in Doctors Hospital looking at the scan.
He pointed out some dark areas in her pelvic area.

"That's cancer," he said, "but I don't know what
kind. We are lucky though, there is a gynecologist
that has an office in the building, she is very good,
and she is on her way here right now."

When the gynecologist arrived and looked at the
scan she said that it was either uterine or ovarian.
She suggested that Martha come to her office where
she could make an examination and we could discuss
what her options were.

After the examination she suggested that Martha

have a complete hysterectomy. She said there was one of the best surgeon's for that operation in the country at the Moffitt Hospital and Cancer Center in Tampa. She said that she would make all of the arrangements for her if Martha wanted her to. She added that Moffitt was among the best in the world. She also said that only after the operation would we know what kind of cancer we were dealing with.

Things moved very fast then. That was over 11 years ago and things are still rather foggy to me. The operation was performed on Thursday, June 29, 1999.

I remember checking into a motel near Moffitt. When I came back I kissed Martha just before she entered the OR (operating room) and then came an agonizing five-and-a-half-hour wait. I believe that *those* five and a half hours were the longest of my life. Periodically, doctors would exit one of the operating rooms to bring news to waiting families. Even without hearing the words, you could read the prognosis on the loved ones faces, 'inoperable,' 'we had to close him (or her) up,' or, 'we got it all,' 'he (or she) is going to be fine.'

I had a lot to think about in the waiting room. It just wasn't fair, I thought, she had only been retired for five years, we had just moved into our dream house and had not even settled in yet.

We were told that the cancer had metastasized, and it was all through her body. They had no idea how long she would live. They said she was in stage three, and at that time the average survival rate for stage three was about three years.

I had always thought that being 11 years older than her, I would be the first to go, and that was the way it should be. Knowing her as I did, I'm sure she could handle this better than I if it was the other way around. But now I thought I had to somehow stay alive so I could be with her to the end. I believed that no one could take better care of her than I could. Thoughts were reeling in my head. If I could only trade places with her, oh God, how can I live without her? I was the one who was now fearful.

Dianne was sitting beside me and I did not want her to see me cry, and I knew I was going to cry, so I got up and went outside. It was a typically beautiful Florida day out and I walked clear to the back of the parking lot and let go.

I looked up into the blue sky and wailed, and screamed as loud as I could. I wailed and screamed until I was hoarse and nothing came out. And then I broke down and cried like I had never cried before. I then realized that I was panicking, I was crying and choking and trying to gasp for breath. I knew that I had to get hold of myself and get back to the waiting room. It was not easy, but after some time, I forced myself to go back.

In the waiting room the surgeon finally came out, took me into a side room and told me that it was ovarian cancer and he thought they got it all except for the affected lymph nodes. She'd been under so long he hadn't felt it was prudent to try to remove the cancerous nodes. Because the cancer had metastasized, her condition was considered terminal, and she should go on a chemotherapy program as soon as possible, he said.

I was sitting next to her holding her hand when she woke up. She was still groggy, but I kissed her so she would know I was there. I don't remember how many days she was in the Intensive Care Unit (ICU) but I do remember her gripping my hand and asking me,

"Please, don't leave me." I assured her that I would *never* leave her.

She wanted me by her side, as long and as often as possible. The hospital staff was terrific; they said I could sleep on a recliner next to her bed. Each morning a group of doctors came in with her surgeon, and he did all the talking. I took that time to rush to my motel room nearby, shave, shower, change clothes and rush back to her side. This went on until she was discharged and I very carefully drove her home. We thought it was best that she sleep alone so I could not disturb her. But she still wanted me near her. Luckily, one of our guest bedrooms was furnished with two single beds, so she insisted we sleep there so I would be beside her, but could not injure her in my sleep.

Her gynecologist arranged for a nurse to see her every day until she could get around by herself. When she could, and could travel, her doctor at Moffitt wanted to see her before she started her chemo program.

At that visit he explained how chemo killed the good cells as well as the bad and would lower her immune system, so she should avoid situations in which she might be exposed to other diseases. He also suggested that she get a wig because, at one time or another, she would probably lose her hair. By getting a wig ahead of time, she could get one very close to her own hair style and color.

On Tuesday, July 27, 1999, I drove her to the Infusion Center at Moffitt for her first of many chemo treatments. The infusion center was a large place, adjacent to the Hospital. We were amazed at how many people were getting chemo that day, and this was taking place in cities every day all over the country, I thought. It was mind boggling when one thought of how many people have cancer all over the world.

In the meantime, I had read that there was a clinic in Evanston, Illinois (the Block Medical Clinic) that, among other things, specialized in proper nutrition for people with cancer.

When I suggested that we go there, at first Martha seemed reluctant. When I suggested that we go for at least one day and see what it was all about … and asked her what did we have to lose? She agreed. So a few days later we flew to Chicago, upgrading to first class in order to avoid as many people as possible who might be ill. I had bought some surgical masks for her to wear on the plane, but soon found out that that was fruitless. To make me feel better, she did put one on for about an hour, but then took it off.

At the Clinic in Evanston (the home of Northwestern University) we found out a lot about nutrition and cancer … and she ordered many vitamins that the clinic suggested, but she was not

interested in their other programs, so we returned to
Osprey.

CHAPTER EIGHTEEN

I NEVER WILL FORGET WHEN HER HAIR FIRST STARTED TO FALL OUT. I was in the kitchen; she had showered and was in the master bath. I heard her cry out and I rushed toward the bath, we met half way ... in the living room.

She was crying when we embraced. With her head on my shoulder, in her one hand she was holding a handful of hair, the other a brush full of hair, and she was sobbing into my shoulder. I did the best I could to calm her and then helped her cut off the remaining hair so she was then able to put her wig on.

For some time now, she had been golfing four times a week, and playing bridge twice a week. Our social life continued as usual in this time. We had long planned on having a New Year's Eve party in our new home and had invited 14 of our very best friends before we knew that she had cancer. It was going to be black tie to usher in the new millennium. I asked her if she wanted to cancel it, but she wouldn't hear of it. We were going to hire a caterer, but Dianne, a very good cook herself, insisted on catering the whole affair. It was a tremendous success and everybody went happily home in the new millennium.

The routine at Moffitt for taking chemo was always the same. Periodically her doctor would take a CAT scan or x-rays and then he would prescribe the kind of chemo he wanted the infusion center to use. We would always meet with her doctor first, and then go to the infusion center with his prescription for the treatment.

But after two years things came to a screeching halt. We went to the doctor in Tampa as usual, but this time he told Martha that there was nothing more he could do for her. We were stunned. I asked him …

"What do we do now?"

"Well, most women go home and make out their will," he said.

I was driving Martha home. Not a word was spoken for many miles. We were both still in shock. Then I suggested that she call our good friend and next door neighbor, Doctor Thane Cody, as soon as we got home.

Dr. Thane Cody, and his wife Joann, had been our next door neighbors now for over two years. When they first moved in I did what I did for most new neighbors—I invited him to golf with me so I could show him around both of our courses, and the clubhouse. I could see that Thane was a very good golfer and suggested that he might want to play with the men's league; I then showed him how to sign up.

When you golf 18 holes with someone as a twosome, you learn a lot about them, and likewise, they learn a lot about you. I learned that Thane was a retired doctor and had been with the Mayo Clinic in Minnesota for 30 years. He had also been on Mayo Clinic's board of directors. When the board decided to build their first satellite in Jacksonville, Florida, the board put Thane in charge of it. He not only built it, he also staffed it, and on that staff was an oncologist by the name of William (Bill) Maples. And this part was most important, Thane said that he, himself, had cancer, and Bill Maples had kept him alive for the past seven years.

Once home, Martha made a beeline for the phone and called Thane, telling him what had just happened. Thane told her that he would call her right back. He did, and said that she had an appointment with his oncologist, Doctor Bill Maples, at the Mayo Clinic in Jacksonville, next Tuesday at 5:30 p.m.

This was the beginning of the most amazing doctor-patient relationship that I have ever witnessed, and will never forget. Doctor Bill Maples has got to be one of the very best doctors out there.

The following day Dr. Maples called Martha and asked her to get her records from Moffitt. When she asked for her records her doctor at Moffitt said that, for some technical reason, he could not give them to her. So she called Doctor Maples, and he called Moffitt, and her records were then transmitted to Doctor Maples immediately.

On Monday we made our first four-and-a-half-hour drive to the Mayo Clinic in Jacksonville. We checked into the Sawgrass Marriott Hotel and on Tuesday drove to the Mayo Clinic in nearby Jacksonville.

We arrived at Dr. Maple's waiting room about 5:15. At 5:30 we were called into his office. This was obviously quitting time for most people for they were pouring out of the clinic when we went into Doctor Maples' office and there wasn't a soul left in his waiting room as we went in.

I was very impressed with his office and I took particular note of his computer; it was a Dell with the largest screen I had ever seen. After meeting the good doctor we watched as he read every page of her stack of records. He took notes and asked her questions as he went along. He finished at 7:30 and swung his chair around to face us. Looking at Martha he said ...

"We have a clinical trial going on right now that I believe you would qualify for, do you want to try it?" And, of course, Martha said yes.

We saw Doctor Maples about once every few months for the next five years. Her visits always included a CAT scan, blood tests and more. We were usually there three or four days and always saw Doctor Maples on the last day there. We never saw him for less than 30 or 40 minutes each visit.

Martha and I learned more about cancer than we ever wanted to know in the seven years she fought the disease. We learned that there are four stages of cancer. Those in stages one and two have the best chance of survival.

As I said before, Martha was in stage three, which means that it had metastasized and spread to the lymph nodes, which is considered terminal. That means eventually it will kill you, if nothing else does first. As far as each individual is concerned, your longevity is just a guess.

Stage four is the worst stage. It means that it has already spread to other vital organs.

Oncologists, periodicals, the Internet, books and

other literature will tell you that ovarian cancer is very difficult, if not impossible, to detect early.

Oncologists compare all resources spent on cancer to a pie, and resources spent on ovarian cancer, when compared to breast cancer, are much smaller. And this makes sense when you consider that, among women, in 2007 approximately 40,598 died from breast cancer as compared to approximately 14,621 from ovarian cancer.

At Moffitt, we were told that they were presently spending most of their resources for ovarian cancer on finding a way to detect it earlier. What we really need, they say, is a much larger pie.

Sometime later, the Codys had to make the four-and-a-half-hour trip more often. They eventually tired of that, then sold their house next door and moved to another golf course community much closer to the clinic. When that happened we would take an extra day to golf and spend more time with our good friends and ex-neighbors whenever we were there. Thane has had two hip replacements since, and I understand that he was still golfing.

CHAPTER NINETEEN

The beginning of the end.

OUR NEXT SCHEDULED APPOINTMENT WITH DOCTOR MAPLES was to be on September 26th and 27th in 2006. When we were making plans for the trip Martha cautioned me not to expect good news. Knowing Martha as I did, that statement really frightened me; something must be happening to her that she was keeping from me.

In the five years under Doctor Maples' care Martha played golf four times a week, and bridge two or three times a week, that is, when we weren't traveling. We managed to attend a dinner with retired Ameritech officers in Chicago each December just before Christmas, and another in Naples, Florida with ex-Telephone Company Officers.

At that time we always spent a week in Chicago and Michigan visiting friends and relatives.

We spent weeks in London, Paris, Brussels, Hawaii (twice), Puerto Rico, Budapest, Vienna and Prague.

On Sunday, July 23, 2006, Martha and I played golf with three other couples that day, and then we all went out for dinner at a local restaurant.

On Sunday, July 30, 2006, Martha and I played golf alone.

On Monday, July 31, 2006, I went with Martha to the infusion center in Sarasota for her chemo, as I always did. Martha had been taking chemo in Sarasota now with Dr. Malarino, under the direction of Dr. Maples in Jacksonville.

On Friday, August 4, 2006, I had lunch with friends at the club. Martha was hosting bridge with her friends and I usually went to the club to get out of their way. Martha was never one to complain, but I was concerned because I noticed that she had been experiencing a shortness of breath lately.

On Sunday, August 6, 2006, we golfed with Dianne and her husband, and then had dinner at J. Ryans, a nearby restaurant.

On Wednesday, August 8, 2006, Martha had her hair done in preparation for our trip to Chicago the next day. My concern was steadily growing because of her shortness of breath.

On Wednesday, August 9, 2006, we flew to Chicago and checked into the Drake as we usually did when in Chicago.

On Thursday, August 10, 2006, we had lunch with an old Chicago friend.

On Friday, August 11, 2006, Martha had lunch with Pat, her long-time secretary; she did this every time we came to Chicago.

On Saturday, August 12, 2006, Martha wanted to go shopping on One Magnificent Mile. Frank and Faye Zimmerman, who had a condo in Chicago, were going to pick us up later and drive us to Dennis and Karen Johnson's house in Barrington for dinner at six o'clock.

Nordstrom's was the farthest store on her route but she intended to stop at others on the way. I was concerned because I had doubts about her being able to make such a trip walking, which she insisted on doing. I had to go along with it though; I just couldn't tell her I didn't think she could make it. We stopped at all of her favorite stores along the way, not necessarily to shop there, but for her to catch her breath. We finally got to Nordstrom's and took the escalator up. She got off at all of her favorite floors and wandered around each one, looking at dresses, price tags and other things, not buying anything.

I had done this with her thousands of times, in this store and others. She always wanted me to go with her when she shopped. Before she bought anything to wear, she always asked me if I liked it. *She never bought anything I did not like.* But she did not buy anything today.

My heart ached. I could not help feeling that she knew that she was doing this for the last time. We took the escalator back to the ground floor and I suggested we take a cab back to the Drake. She quietly agreed, and we caught a cab. She never said a word on the way back; my heart was aching so bad I could barely hold back the tears.

Oh how I loved her! We had always loved each other, but in the last seven years a bond, a bond like no other, had developed between us. I couldn't possibly count the many times I thought that there was something terribly wrong here; I should be the one in her shoes.

We had a wonderful dinner with our old friends In Barrington. As always, when we got together after dinner we had cocktails and took pictures. They were the last pictures ever taken of the love of my life. She was so beautiful. She smiled often, never mentioned her physical problems earlier in the day and engaged in conversations as if nothing was wrong.

Our friends weren't aware of it, but I knew that this was, in all probability, the last time they would ever see one of their very best friends, alive. In the meantime I couldn't say a thing, and it was breaking my heart.

CHAPTER TWENTY

BACK AT THE OAKS Martha was still experiencing a shortness of breath under exertion. The next time she saw Doctor Mallarino, Martha told her what was happening.

The doctor took her out of her office and asked her to walk the hallways until she was short of breath. When she stopped, Doctor Mallarino took her pulse and listened to her heart. Back in the office she suggested that she see a cardiologist. Martha agreed, and the good doctor set up an appointment for her with a Doctor Bredlau.

On August 28th we saw Doctor Bredlau. He examined her and suggested that she take a stress test. The test was scheduled for September 1st. On the 1st she passed the test with flying colors and Doctor Bredlau said that there was nothing wrong with her heart.

A few days before we were to leave for Jacksonville Martha told me, again, not to expect good news. This to me was a *very* bad sign. I mentioned it to our good friends John and Mary Blutenthal, and John insisted on driving us. He said if it was bad news, he didn't want me driving her home alone.

Also, he had a daughter that lived near the Sawgrass Marriott, and he would be able to spend some time with her.

On Wednesday, the 27th, Martha took a CAT

scan in the morning and was scheduled to see Dr. Maples in the afternoon. When we entered his office that afternoon he embraced Martha and then told her there was nothing more he could do for her. She then asked …

"How much time do I have?" He said, "A month, perhaps two." After telling her how sorry he was, and that she was the most courageous patient he ever had, he suggested that she talk to Doctor Mallarino about Hospice.

Back at the Marriott we entered our room and broke into tears. We embraced and, sobbing in my ear, she said …

"I didn't want to leave you. I love you."

"I love you too, and I never, ever, wanted you to leave me," I said. True to his word John drove us home on the 28th.

Friday, September 29, 2006, was our thirty-ninth wedding anniversary. That evening we had dinner at one of our favorite restaurants, Ophelia's. Ophelia's is on Siesta Key, right on the waterfront. We had celebrated many anniversary dinners there in the past, and just a few months ago we had decided to celebrate our fortieth there.

There was no celebration tonight; it was a very solemn dinner. We sat holding hands at our favorite table where we could see young people traversing the bay in kayaks at sundown. Directly across the bay we could see our beloved 'Oaks.'

Martha, with tears in her eyes and anguish in her voice, said …

"We'll never see our fortieth."

***

Monday, October 2nd, she had her hair done as usual and Tuesday she saw Doctor Mallareno about Hospice. She went in the doctor's office alone. I waited in the waiting room.

On Friday we went to see a movie with our good friends Jack and Betty Lukanich, and things went downhill from there on.

A male nurse arrived from Hospice on October 9th. He wanted all of her medications and later replaced them with those supplied by Hospice. Also, about that time, she was starting to feel some pain in her back. The nurse then put her on Oxycodone. Gradually the pain in her back was increasing and the nurse ordered her a hospital bed. It was delivered later that day. We set it up next to our bed in the master bedroom. The next day Ernie Bernanches, a friend with a wheel chair, brought it to the house.

Every day the pain seemed to get worse and on Friday the 20th of October the nurse said that he was going out of town for the weekend and when he came back next Monday Martha might want to consider going to Hospice where he said they had more powerful pain killers that he could not use. He said that when they had her pain under control she could return home.

Saturday afternoon, October 21st, after breakfast Martha was sitting in her recliner. The television was on but she wasn't watching it. She had a small lap blanket over her legs and was carefully making notes from a Bobbi Brown makeup booklet on a 5x7 lined pad.

I had just made the beds and was busy cleaning up the kitchen; Dianne and her husband were due any minute. I didn't think much of it at the time, but she had apparently finished her notes and tore them from the pad, then handed them to me just as the door bell rang, saying;

"Here, have Di go to Saks and get me these," and I read her list she had been working so hard on:

Intensive Skin Care #45
Loose Powder – Warm 6
(or a shade lighter)
Foundation #4

I have those original notes in front of me now. She had labored over them for almost an hour trying to pick out exactly what she wanted.

I have in front of me another note she left behind, but you have to know that Martha was a stickler for sending thank you notes as well as birthday and Christmas cards.

When it came to birthday cards she had a list of all of our relatives and about every friend we had. Some days we could actually spend the whole day looking for just the right birthday cards, because they had to say just the right thing.

The notes in front of me now were meant to be for thank you cards and were made the last days of her life.

<u>Marcia</u>
>   2 nightey [*she meant nities*]
>   2 robes

Soup Terry
3Soups Betty
Soup Barb

Flowers - Tom & Linda
Flowers - John & Mary
Flowers - Mark & Cathy

Ernie - Wheel Chair

For those who say she knew she wasn't coming back from Hospice, and there were some, I say, hogwash. I spent too many times at Saks watching her buy makeup, and, besides, there is nobody that knew her better than I! And I believe she knew exactly what she was doing. I don't know much about makeup, but why would she want makeup if she didn't think she would need it? Or, be here to send thank you cards? That just wasn't the Martha I knew.

I am convinced that she, just as I, really believed the nurse when he said that when Hospice had her pain under control she could come home. As I have said many times, my wife was an eternal optimist, and when Doctor Maples said one or two months, all she heard was the "two." I have asked this question of myself many times. Why shouldn't we have believed the nurse? Were we supposed to have known that he was lying?

Sunday morning, October 22nd, we knew that Dianne and her husband were coming over in the afternoon, so I helped Martha into the wheelchair and took her to her recliner in the family room where she could watch television while I made breakfast and the beds.

Then we both watched the PGA tournament, as we always did on Sundays. Dianne arrived late that afternoon, followed by Betty and Jack. They were all there when a replacement nurse arrived.

When the nurse asked Martha how bad her pain was on a scale of one to ten, she said it was a five or six. When she was asked if she wanted to go to Hospice she said "yes."

I had not expected this and was shocked. I had thought that this should happen tomorrow, when the male nurse came back. There was nothing I could say though; she was the one in pain.

After making a phone call the nurse said that one room was available at the Hospice at 5957 Rand Road in Sarasota.

Late Sunday evening, the nurse led a small caravan of cars out of The Oaks and headed for the Hospice House on Rand Road. Believing that she would be coming back after her pain was under control, we were not aware that this would be Martha's last ride. As it turned out, Martha would never again see her home, or The Oaks Club she loved so much.

The Hospice nurse led the way. She was in the first car and the rest of us followed. It was dark when we arrived at the Rand Road Hospice House. A wheel chair was brought out for Martha and they wheeled her into room 12.

Room 12 is a very large room; I was very impressed. To your left as you enter the room is a large stuffed chair facing the bed, the head of the bed is against the wall in the middle of the room to your right. The entrance to the bathroom is to your right.

A very large couch is on the far wall facing the bed. They offered to bring a small bed in for me but I told them I wanted to spend my nights on the couch. That way I could see the whole room—the bed, the doorway and even most of the living room.

The living room was carpeted, with a grand piano in the far corner. Scattered around the room were couches, stuffed chairs, end tables, lamps and even a card table, complete with chairs.

After everyone left that first night a nurse brought me a blanket and pillow. Then Martha was given some kind of medication, which I assumed was a painkiller or sleeping pill.

She appeared to be fine, so I told her I loved her. We did our customary good night kiss and I went to sleep on the couch expecting to see her in the morning. Little did I know at the time that, after over 43 years, that kiss would be our last.

About three in the morning I awoke to hear a commotion near the doorway of room 12, leading to the living room. The only light in the room came from the bathroom; the rest of the room, including my couch, was pitch black.

I was somewhat disorientated but could see the nurse's aide struggling with Martha in the doorway to the living room about 15 feet from her bed. As he struggled with her to get her in bed she cried …

"You're hurting me," and … "I only wanted to see my husband." As things turned out, those were the last words my true love would ever speak. It was our first night there and something had gone terribly wrong. As a matter of fact we had only been there about five hours.

Things happened so fast then. The next thing I knew Martha was in bed and a nurse was giving her an injection. By now I was wide awake and I rushed to her side, passing the two as they left. As they passed me they didn't say a word. They just disappeared behind me. At the time my only concern was for my wife. When I got to her she was out like a light. That must have been one potent shot.

Looking back on it, years later, it seems to me it doesn't take a rocket scientist to figure out what probably happened. When she woke up in a strange room the only light was coming from the bathroom and living room, the rest of the room was pitch dark, and I was sleeping on the couch in the corner of the far wall on the other side of the room from the bed.

Evidently she woke up and looked around for me but couldn't see me. She knew that I was there somewhere. The living room was well lit. She saw all those couches out there and most likely thought that I was somewhere out there on one of them. So she started out to find me. What torments me to this day is that there must have been something she wanted to say to me. And now I will never know what it was. I believe that this whole thing could have been avoided if they had just sought my help. Didn't they know I was there? And, if not, why not?

But it's over now, and nothing can bring her back. She died five days later at 6:40 a.m. on October 27, 2006, without ever waking up. And what I have to live with is that less than eight hours before she was knocked out with a shot that she would never come out of ... she was sitting in her recliner, in her own family room, watching a golf tournament with me.

If you've read Part One of this book, can you believe that a woman, who testified to a United States Select Senate Committee as an expert in ... of all things *health care* ... would die this way? Whatever happened to dignity?

By no means do I think that she should have been treated better than anyone else, but I do think that something went terribly wrong here. I am sure that this was not Hospice's normal method of procedure.

That scene in room 12 will forever haunt me.

CHAPTER TWENTY-ONE

SO ... HOW DO I COPE WITH THE LOSS OF MY DEAR WIFE? Five years after her death I find that there are no simple answers. *EVERY case is different!* I don't think I'm doing as good a job as others have here at The Oaks, but having read four books on the subject I highly recommend the suggestion of keeping a journal. I did, and in my case, I'm glad I did. I could never have written this book if I had not done it.

Martha possessed amazing abilities, and was truly a woman of great wisdom. Under any circumstance in public, she was always cool, calm and collected. Once out of the house one would never know she had terminal cancer, or anything else for that matter. During that time, at dances we danced up a storm, played Bingo and went to wine tasting dinners and played competitive golf.

She was the best wife any man could hope for. I adored her and worshiped the ground she walked on. And, in the last seven years my heart bled for her. I agonized over the very thought of losing her, but I knew that I could never show it, for on our first trip to Mayo Clinic I read this story in some booklet lying around the waiting room and I tried to live by it. It went something like this ...

There was a woman who had cancer and her husband was always fawning all over her. Then one day they had an argument and she was delighted, she thought, "He really doesn't think I'm going to die, or he never would have said those things." The object of the story was that people with cancer just want to live a normal life.

I loved Martha more than anything else in this world. She was my true love and my soul mate. My only regret is that I could not trade places with her at the end.

I often say that I was the luckiest man in the world on September 29, 1967, when I married Martha Hall. But perhaps I should thank my lucky stars for that snowstorm in Detroit …

Epilogue

Martha L. Thornton's Career:

Bright, quick, articulate and attractive says Frank Zimmerman. He was so right. But the woman I knew was all of that and more. She was my rock, she knew me like a book. She sensed how hard it was on me while writing the "Blues," a tale I could not talk about. If it was not for her keen perception and understanding of the stress I was going through, there never would have been a "Blues."

In our lifetime relationship, she was the glue that kept me from unraveling. In all of the years I knew her I never saw her lose her composure or her compassion for others. She was truly an amazing and remarkable lady.

On December 15, 1963, she was the first female in the history of the Michigan Bell Telephone Company to be hired in their new management program. She was hired as a *Group Chief Operator-Trainee*.

On June 21, 1964, she became an official *Group Chief Operator*.

On July 03, 1966, she was promoted to *Chief Operator*.

On September 29, 1967, she married Robert L. Thornton.

On July 01, 1971, she made history again by becoming the first *female* in Michigan Bell to become a *District Traffic Manager*.

On December 01, 1974, she became the first *female* to hold the job of *Division Manager of Operating Services Detroit Metro-East*.

On March 01, 1977, she became the first *female* to become the *General Manager of Operating Services*, a statewide position with a budget in excess of 100 million dollars annually, with a staff of 5,000 plus people.

In 1981 she was the first *female* to be named an *Assistant Vice President* of Michigan Bell.

On January 01, 1984, she became the first *female* to become a *Vice President* of Ameritech, the holding company of five telephone companies, Illinois Bell, Ohio Bell, Michigan Bell, Indiana Bell and Wisconsin Bell, when Ameritech became one of the seven "Baby Bells."

On July 05, 1989, the *Wall Street Journal* announced that Martha L. Thornton had been named as *Senior Vice President* of Ameritech. She served in that capacity until she retired in 1994.

From 1990 until 1994 she served on the board of the *Old Kent Financial Corporation.*

In 1990, in Washington, she testified before a select Senate Committee chaired by Senator Ted Kennedy regarding Health Care.

I have in my possession thank you letters from *George W. Bush, Senator Ted Kennedy, Senator Paul Simon, Lynn Martin, former Secretary of Labor in President George H. Bush's Administration and Mayor Harold Washington, Mayor of Chicago.*

During her career she was a lifetime member of the *NAACP.* She was also active in the *Human Resources Management Association of Chicago*, serving as *Vice President* and *President* of that association.

As a member of the *Midwest Business Group* she served as *Vice Chair of the Board.*

When *Senior Vice President* of Ameritech she became a member of The *U.S. Chambers Employers Council on Health Care* and served on the *Executive Board* of the *Center for Telecommunications* at the *University of Southern California* and the *Chicago Network.*

Dianne Hall

Dianne is now a retired Lawyer and CPA living in Florida. I depend on her as I would a partner. She is almost as smart as her mother ... and that is the highest compliment I can bestow on anyone. She has been a great help in co-authoring this book. I don't know what I would do without her.

CPSIA information can be obtained at www.ICGtesting.com
Printed in the USA
LVOW120330200212

269382LV00001B/2/P

9 781933 817743